Microeconomics: Principles and Practices

Dr. David F. Spigelman

Test 1
Chapters 2-7

Copyright © 2010 by David F. Spigelman

All rights reserved. No part of this publication may be reproduced, stored in a retrieval system, or transmitted in any form or by any means, electronic, mechanical, photocopying, recording or otherwise without the express written consent of the author. Printed in the United States. For information on obtaining permission for use of this work, please contact the author care of University of Miami, Department of Economics, 517Q Jenkins Building, Coral Gables, FL 33124.

Microeconomics: Principles and Practices

Table of Contents

Part 1 – The Basics

Ch. 1 Introduction: Why Study Microeconomics?
Ch. 2 The Production Function and the Gains from Specialization
Ch. 3 Basics of Supply and Demand
Ch. 4 The Elasticity of Demand, Supply and Income

Part 2 – The Consumer

Ch. 5 Consumer Choice under Conditions of Scarcity
Ch. 6 Consumer Surplus, Producer Surplus and Welfare Analysis
Ch. 7 Income and Substitution Effects and Consumer Choice

Part 3 – The Firm and Market Structure

Ch. 8   Production Costs, Revenues and Profit
Ch. 9   Perfect Competition
Ch. 10 Monopoly
Ch. 11 Oligopoly and Strategic Behavior by Firms
Ch. 12 Monopolistic Competition

Part 4 – The Labor Market

Ch. 13 The Labor Market, Human Capital and Productivity

Part 5 – Taxation and the Public Sector

Ch. 14 Taxation Policy: Efficiency vs. Equity
Ch. 15 Government and the Market for Goods
Ch. 16 Externalities and their Remedies

Part 6 – International Trade

Ch. 17 International Trade

ACKNOWLEDGEMENTS

This book is dedicated to my family: my wife Meryl, daughters Mia and Kayla, and my son Jacob. They are my inspiration in everything I do.

    I would like to thank Michael Gotterer for able research and editorial assistance. It would be impossible to find a more dedicated, competent and intelligent assistant. Michael was helpful in every aspect of the writing process.

Chapter 1

Introduction: Why Study Microeconomics?

Economics is the study of the allocation of scarce resources. While macroeconomics explores the larger units in the overall economy like consumer spending, government spending and fluctuations in national income or gross domestic product (GDP), microeconomics focuses on smaller economic units such as the individual, the firm and/or an individual industry. There are many interesting policy questions that we can gain insight into using microeconomic theory.

For example, many people tend to assume that taxes fall most heavily on an individual buying an item that is being taxed. However, we will see that the incidence of a tax—i.e., the burden from a tax—may not fall on the consumer of an item under certain circumstances even though the tax is paid by him or her at the register. As another example where people's presumptions can be wrong, many people believe that the corporate income tax falls most heavily on wealthy people, presumably the owners of public companies through their stock holdings. However, evidence tends to suggest that capital is mobile and seeks its highest possible return around the world. Working class individuals may, in fact, be the most adversely impacted segment of the population if high marginal tax rates cause investment flows to leave the United States. Having less capital to work with would lower the productivity (or output per unit of labor) of the American work force and this would tend to lead to lower wages in a capitalist economy where workers are paid in accordance with their productivity.

Questions about the incidence of taxes are very relevant to the most important policy issues that are being discussed at the present time. As health reform is being debated in the US Congress, President Obama has proposed that insurance companies be taxed for offering overly inclusive health insurance to wealthy people. We will find that we cannot predict who bears the burden of this tax—health insurance companies or wealthy individuals—until we study something called the elasticity of demand and supply for health insurance. We will find in our studies that the incidence of the tax will fall most heavily on the party—supplier or consumer of health services—that has the most inelastic supply or demand.

These are just a few of the possible applications of microeconomic theory. The issues that can be addressed using microeconomic theory are widespread and enter into almost all aspects of human behavior as it pertains to the marketplace, including the markets for goods, labor, capital and human capital.

The text is oriented toward a graphical and problem-solving approach. There will be a set of suggested problems at the end of each chapter. The author suggests students try to work through the problems as much as possible. Students learn to solve basic problems using economic reasoning and analytical tools.

Chapter 2

The Production Function and the Gains from Specialization

In microeconomics, firms are the economic entities that produce goods and services, generally referred to as output. It is useful to think of the ability of a nation's firms to produce output as the "production function" for the nation. A simple production could be written in functional form as:

$$Y = f(K, L, T)$$

where Y is the output (or real GDP for the economy—more about this later), K is defined as the total available capital in an economy which for our purposes will consist of all the non-labor, non-technology inputs to the production process—i.e., the physical and raw material inputs to the production process, L is defined as the labor inputs to the production process which could be thought of as man-hours or "people-hours" of labor per month or per year, and T which represents the human capital or technology-related inputs to the production process.

Let us imagine an economy, Country A, that only produces two types of goods: agricultural goods and manufactured goods. Of course, this is an oversimplification of the true nature of most nation's economies, but often we use simple models to gain insight into a more complex world and that is what will be doing throughout this text. A model should be simple enough to be able to build it in a reasonable amount of time, but complex enough to gain insights into the economic system that we are endeavoring to understand.

Supposing that the country can put all of its resources into the production of manufactured goods, all of its resources into the production of agricultural goods, or can flexibly alter the percentage of resources that it puts into one activity or the other, we may arrive at a production function that looks like Figure 2.1 below.

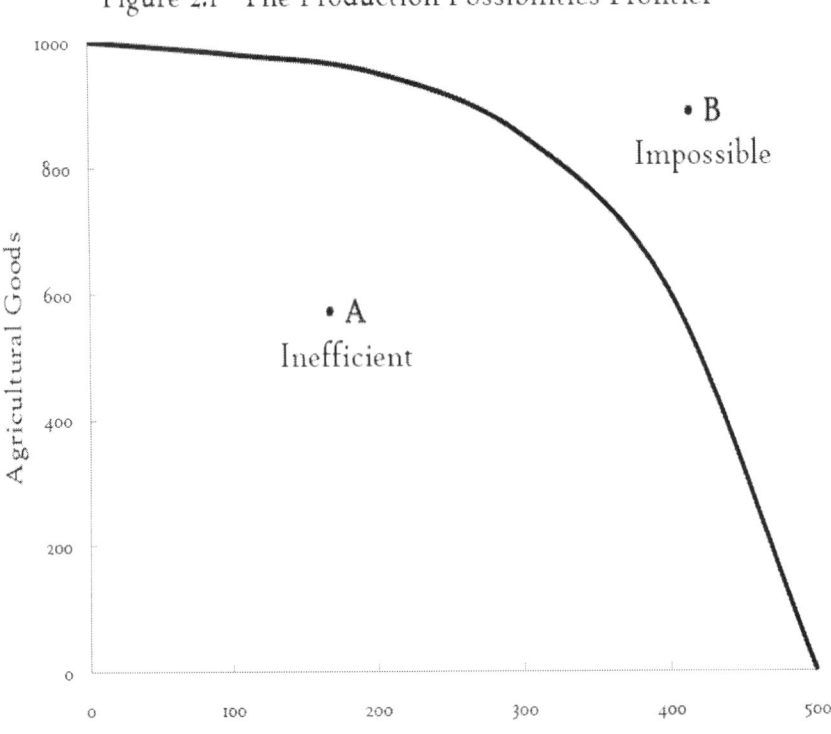
Figure 2.1 The Production Possibilities Frontier

If Country A puts all of its resources into the production of agricultural goods, it can produce 1000 tons of grain per year. On the other hand, if it puts all of its resources into the production of manufactured goods, it can produce 500 manufactured items per year. Notice that the production function for Country A has a "bowed out" shape. The reason that we portray Country A's production function as having a bowed out shape is because normally a country would experience something called ***diminishing returns*** to its factors of production. This is because some inputs to the production process might be better suited to the production of one good relative to the other. For example, some workers might be more experienced in agricultural production than in manufacturing. Thus, if all workers are at first devoted to manufacturing, and we gradually take workers out of manufacturing and shift resources toward agricultural production, at first we would take the workers that are more skilled at agricultural production. At first we would get a big boost to agricultural production without much of a loss to manufacturing output. But as we shifted more resources toward agriculture, eventually we would be taking some of the resources best suited to manufacturing and moving them toward the agricultural sector. Therefore, we will begin to experience diminishing returns to the factors of production and would experience a bigger and bigger loss to manufacturing output relative to the smaller and smaller gains in agricultural output.

Generally, we expect the principle of diminishing returns to apply to all of the factors of production, but especially to capital (K) and labor (L). In the discussion of comparative advantage to ensue in this text, we will portray the production functions of different countries as linear, but this is mainly to make the computations easier.

We call the graph of the production function like the one in Figure 2.1 a "production possibilities frontier." It maps out all the possible points where an economy could produce using all the available factors of production. The economy could produce at a point like A, but it would be inefficient to produce there; i.e., it would not effectively employ all fo the factors of production to produce that level of output.

It might be desirable to produce at a point like B, but that would not be possible with the current availability of the factors of production. Therefore, point B is not a possible choice for production at the present time. In the future, with growth in one or more of the factors of production or with the advent of improved technology, point B might become attainable, but it is not at present.

COMPARATIVE ADVANTAGE AND THE GAINS FROM TRADE

Let us suppose now that there are two countries: Country A and Country B. Suppose also that these countries produce only two goods, wheat and laptop computers. Production schedules for the two countries are given in Table 2.1 below:

Table 2.1

Country A		Country B	
Wheat (tons)	Laptop Computers	Wheat (tons)	Laptop
0	100	0	50
100	90	100	45
200	80	200	40
300	70	300	35
400	60	400	30
500	50	500	25
600	40	600	20
700	30	700	15
800	20	800	10
900	10	900	5
1000	0	1000	0

In this simple example, Country A can exchange resources between the production of laptop computers with the following tradeoff: 10 tons of wheat for 1 laptop computer. Thus, the **opportunity cost** of producing laptops, or how much Country A gives up to produce one laptop computer, is 10 tons of wheat. For Country B, the opportunity cost of a laptop computer is 20 tons of wheat.

Figure 2.2 The Production Possibilities Frontier for Countries A and B

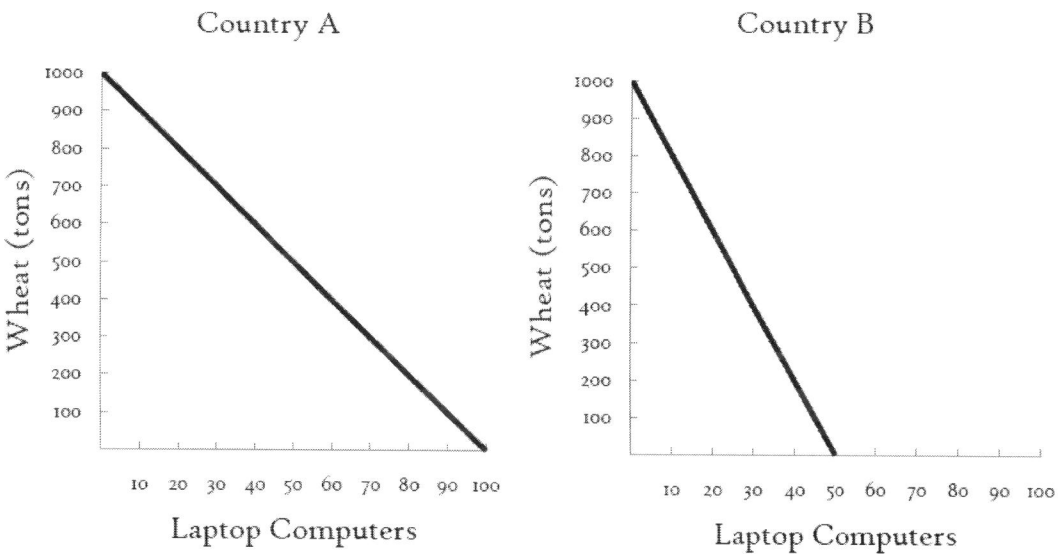

Now, let's define a few useful concepts that we will work with:

Absolute advantage – we say a country has an absolute advantage in producing a good if it can make more of the good using available factors of production.

Comparative advantage – we say a country has a comparative advantage in producing a good if it has a lower opportunity cost of what it as to give up to produce that good.

Therefore, in the example above neither country has an absolute advantage in the production of wheat because both countries can make the same amount of wheat if they use all of their resources in producing wheat. Country A has an absolute advantage in the production of laptop computers because it can make more laptop computers. Country A also has a comparative advantage in the production of laptop computers, while Country B has a comparative advantage in the production of wheat. This is because for Country A, the opportunity cost of producing wheat is relatively higher whereas for Country B the opportunity cost of producing wheat is relatively lower. The concept of comparative advantage looks solely at the relative tradeoffs of producing the different items. As long as the ratios are different in terms of how one good can be exchanged for another, with two goods, one country will always have a comparative advantage in the production of one good and the other country will have a comparative advantage in the production of the other good.

The reason we are interested in studying these relationships is because the idea of comparative advantage gives rise to the insight that countries can improve their well-being by tending to specialize in the production of the goods in which they have a comparative advantage and trading for the goods where they don't have the comparative advantage. For example, in the simple example herein, in autarky (i.e., without any trade), suppose each country uses half of its resources to produce wheat and half to produce laptop computers. Output would be as follows:

	Country A	Country B	Total
Laptop Computers	50	25	75
Tons of Wheat	500	500	1000

If Country A were to specialize in the production of laptop computers and Country B were to specialize in the production of wheat, one can see that the two countries would be able to produce the same quantity of wheat, 1000 tons, but a greater quantity of laptop computers – 100, instead of 75.

In autarky, the price ratio of the two goods would be determined by the rate at which production could be exchanged between the two goods, one laptop for 10 tons of wheat in Country A and one laptop for 20 tons of wheat in Country B. Thus, in autarky the price of a computer relative to a ton of wheat in Country A would be 10:1 versus 20:1 in Country B.

With trade, a price ratio could be established between the price ratios in the individual countries that would enable the two countries to reach a higher level of consumption of laptop computers with the same level of consumption of wheat. See Figure 2.3 below.

Figure 2.3

Country A

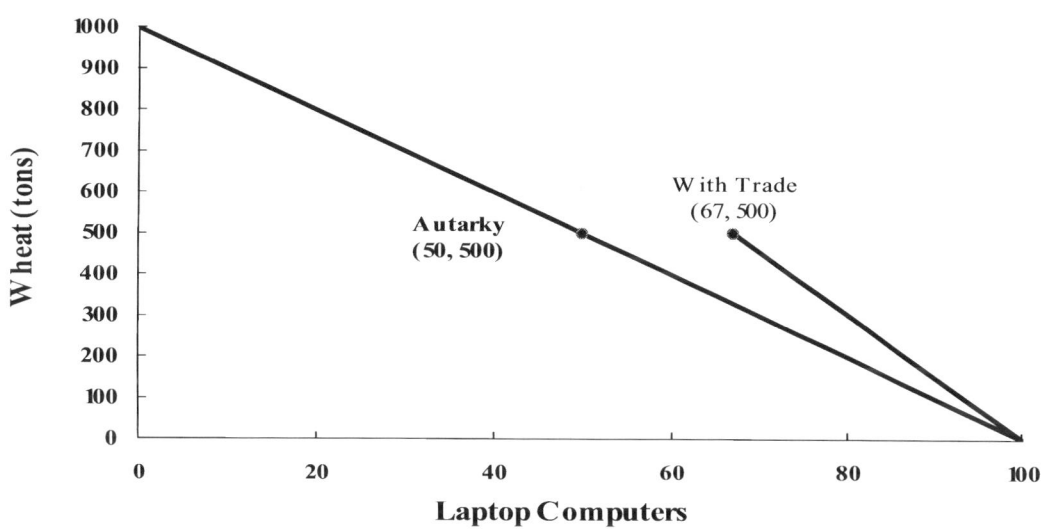

Country B

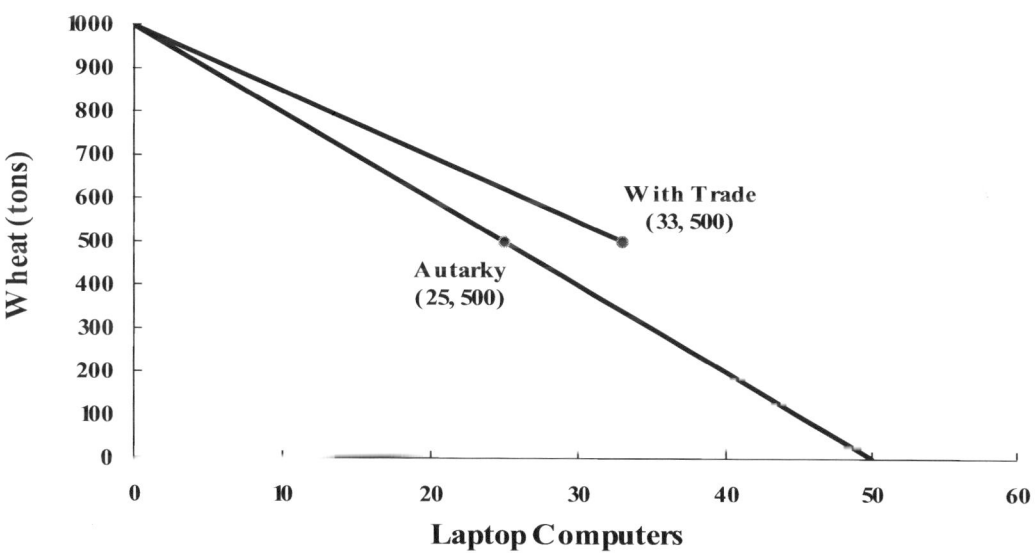

In this example, Country A produces only laptop computers and trades 33 laptop computers for 500 tons of wheat. Country B produces only wheat. The price ratio would have to be between 20:1 and 10:1, the price ratios in autarky. In this way, both countries can get to a more desirable outcome: more laptop computers and the same number of tons of wheat.

Thus, we can see that because of comparative advantage and through specialization of labor, the countries are able to realize gains from trade-- even if one country has an absolute advantage in the production of both goods! As long as the slope of the production possibility frontier is different in the two countries, there will be the possibility of generating gains from trade through specialization due to the principle of comparative advantage.

Practice Problems for Chapter 2

1. Suppose a group of one hundred students is assigned two tasks: a) producing a leaflet extolling the virtues of the university they are attending to distribute to prospective students, or b) cooking a Thanksgiving dinner and serving it to homeless people as a gesture of goodwill on behalf of their university. Draw a production possibilities curve for this "economy." How do you think it should be shaped? Do you think there will be diminishing marginal returns to labor in the production of either good or both goods?

2. Suppose Japan and South Korea produce only two goods: a) rice and b) cars. Given the following information and assuming each country has 100 million workers, answer the questions that follow.

	Japan		South Korea	
Millions of Workers In Rice Production	Rice per Month(pm) (millions of tons)	Cars pm (millions)	Rice pm (million)	Cars pm (millions)
0	0	10	0	20
10	100	9	100	18
20	200	8	200	16
30	300	7	300	14
40	400	6	400	12
50	500	5	500	10
60	600	4	600	8
70	700	3	700	6
80	800	2	800	4
90	900	1	900	2
100	1000	0	1000	0

a) Which country has an absolute advantage in the production of cars? Of rice? Which country has the comparative advantage in the production of each good?

b) What is the opportunity cost of one million cars in South Korea? In Japan? What is the opportunity cost of 10 million bushels of wheat in South Korea? In Japan?

c) Draw the production possibilities curves for Japan and South Korea.

d) Propose an allocation of labor for each country and explain how the two countries can improve their total consumption through trade. What do you think will happen to the price ratio for rice relative to the price of cars with trade? What is the maximum and minimum for the price ratio?

Chapter 3

Basics of Supply and Demand

Many people—even those who have never taken an economics class—have heard of the "law of supply and demand." In quite simple terms, the law of supply and demand says that when many people want more of a good, its price will tend to rise, and when many people decide to sell a good, its price will tend to fall. We are going to formally model this phenomenon and will use these basic ideas throughout the text.

Let's start with the demand curve. Demand curves tend to be downward sloping, but not always. The reason demand curves are downward sloping is because, when graphing P (price) on the y-axis and Q_d (quantity demanded) on the x-axis, when P falls more people are willing to buy a good. Conversely, if we were to start with a low price and gradually increase the price, as the price rises, fewer and fewer people would b willing to buy the good.

A simple demand curve for bicycles is graphed below in Figure 3.1

Figure 3.1
Demand for Bicycles

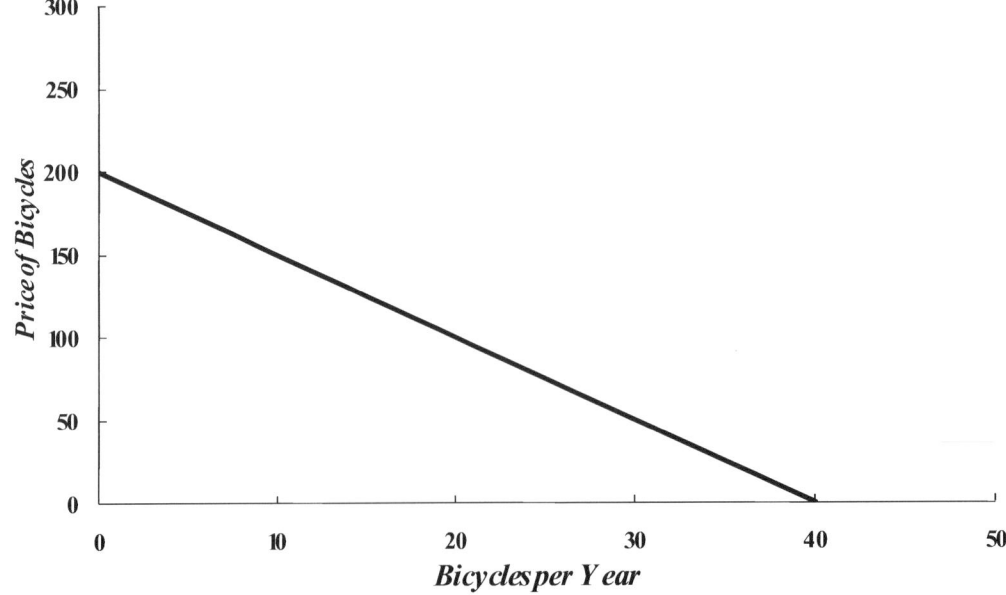

In the graph above, when the price of a bicycle is $200, the quantity demanded is zero. We use the term "quantity demanded" when we are referring to a point on the demand curve or when we are referring to a movement along the curve. When we are referring to a shift in the curve itself, we use the term "change in demand," as opposed to the term quantity demanded.

As a general rule, when something shifts that represents a variable that is not on the axes, and that affects demand, those changes will tend to be represented by a shift in the demand curve.

In Table 3.1 below, we list some of the things that can shift the demand curve, either up or down.

Table 3.1

Things that Shift the Demand Curve Up and to the Right	**Things that Shift the Demand Curve Down and to the Left**
1) An increase in per capita income	1) A decrease in p.c. income
2) Active lifestyles become popular	2) Fitness becomes less important
3) A trend among people to "go green"	3) A drop in fuel prices
4) An increase in fuel prices	
5) An increase in automobile congestion in an area with adequate bike paths	

Figure 3.2
A Change That Shifts the Demand Curve to the Right

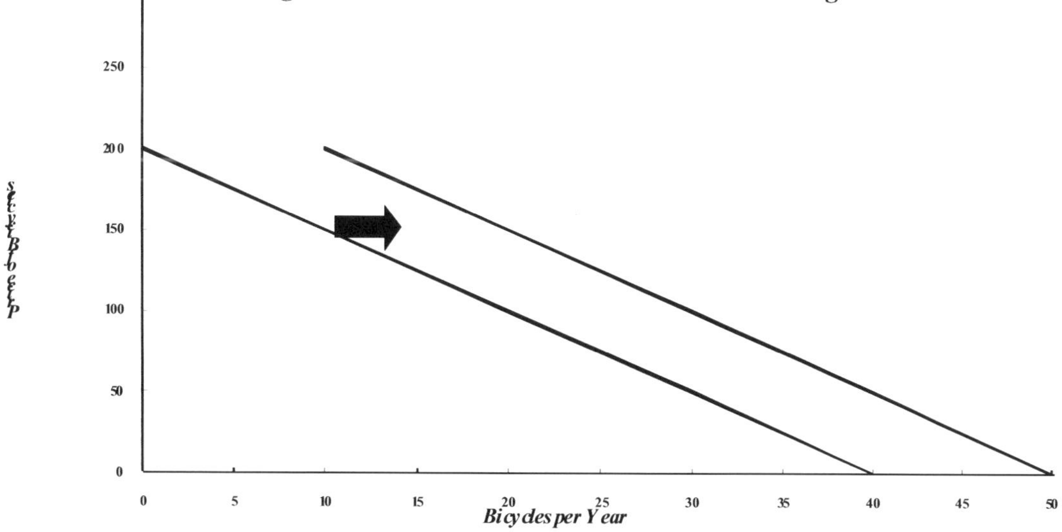

Generally, most of the changes that would shift the demand curve to the right, the opposite of these changes would tend to shift the demand curve to the left.

As demand curves mostly slope downward, supply curves usually slope upward. Suppliers usually need to be enticed with a higher price to encourage them to produce more. In Figure 3.3 below, we see that an increase in the price leads to an increase in the "quantity supplied."

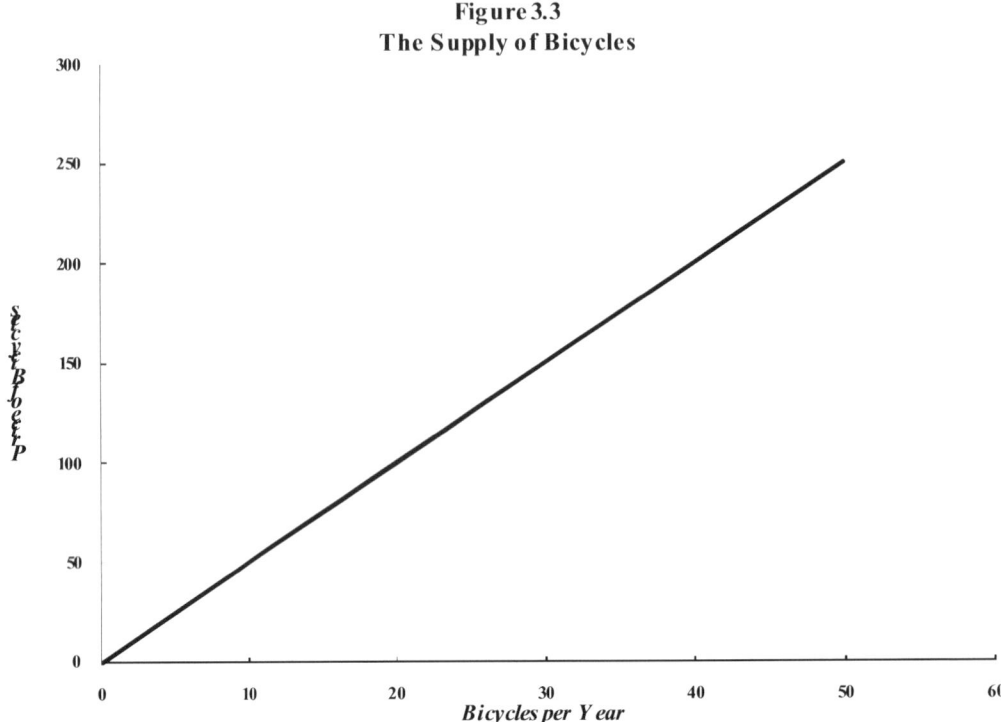

Figure 3.3
The Supply of Bicycles

We use a similar lexicon when speaking of supply. Again, we use the term "quantity supplied" when speaking of a point on the supply curve or when we move along the curve we speak of a change in the quantity supplied.

Similarly, something must change which is not on one of the axes that affects supply in order for there to be a "change in supply" in which case the curve itself shifts. Figure 3.4 illustrates a shift in the supply curve to the right.

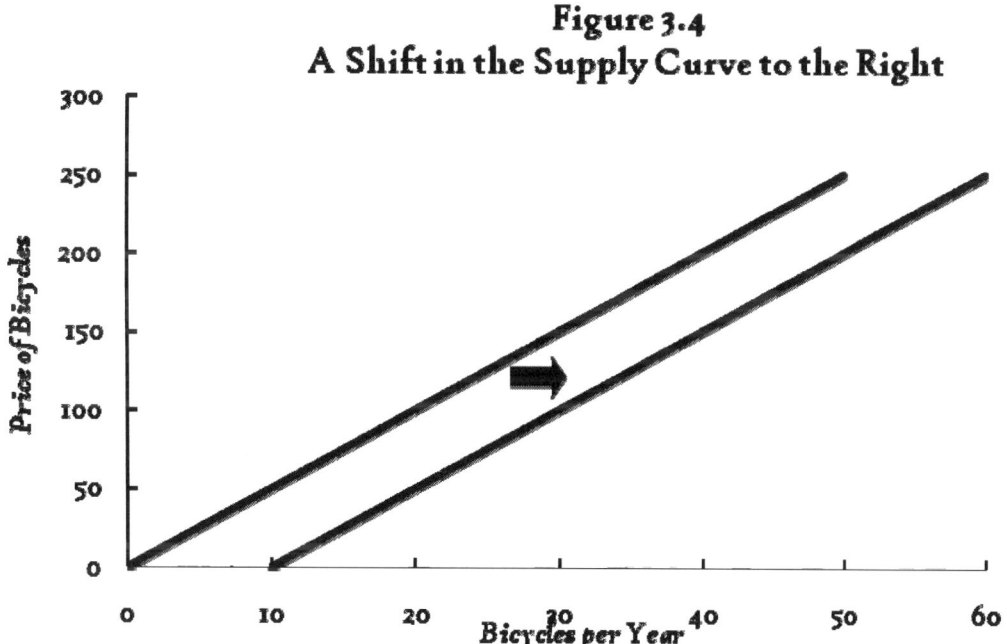

Table 3.2

Things that Shift the Supply Curve Down and to the Right

1) A drop in the price of raw materials
2) An expected drop in prices
3) An improvement in technology that reduces the cost of making bikes

Things that Shift the Supply Curve Up and to the Left

1) An increase in rm prices
2) Anticipated rise in bike prices

Finally, in Figure 3.5 below, we combine the supply and demand curves to arrive at the equilibrium price and quantity for bicycles. If we had equations for the supply and demand curves, we could set $Q_d = Q_s$ and solve for the equilibrium price and quantity. In Fig. 3.5 below, the equilibrium price is $100 and the equilibrium quantity is 20 (million) bicycles per year.

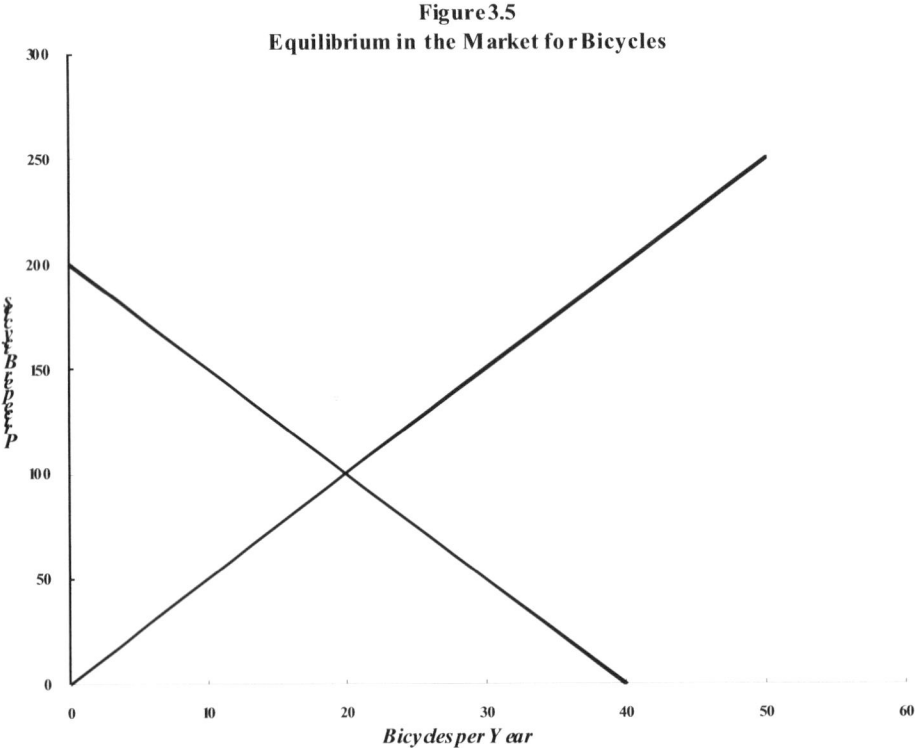

3.5

Practice Problems for Chapter 3

1. Draw simple supply and demand curves for the market for collectible baseball cards (in terms of the average price for a traded baseball card during a year). Show what would happen to the equilibrium price in the market given the following changes:

    a) Several Hollywood stars catch the collecting bug leading to an increase in the popularity of collecting
    b) An increase in the cost of raw materials leads to an increase in baseball card production costs
    c) A decrease in leisure time leads to a decrease in the popularity of baseball card trading
    d) A large collector of baseball cards decides that prices are likely to fall in the future and moves to sell his collection

2. Given the following supply and demand curves for cellular phones, graph the supply and demand curves:

    $Q_d = 300 - 2P$

    $Q_s = 3P$

    where P is the price in dollars and Q is the quantity demanded of cellphones sold per year.

    a) Find the equilibrium price and quantity that clears the market for cellular phones.

    b) What would happen to the equilibrium price and quantity if the demand curve changed to $Q_d = 250 - 2P$?

    c) Can you name a few reasons that might have caused this shift in the demand curve?

Chapter 4

The Elasticity of Demand, Supply and Income

In this chapter, we introduce a new concept – "elasticity". What economists really mean by elasticity is responsiveness. Let's start with the elasticity of demand. Verbally, we define the elasticity of demand as the (absolute value of the) percentage change in quantity demanded for a percentage change in price. Mathematically, we are going to employ a technique known as the "midpoint method" to calculate percentage changes. The formula for elasticity of demand is given as:

4.1 $\varepsilon = |[(Q_{D2} - Q_{D1})/\{(Q_{D1} + Q_{D2})/2\}] \div [(P_2 - P_1)/\{(P_1 + P_2)/2\}]|$

where "ε" (the Greek letter epsilon) will be our symbol for the elasticity of demand. Similarly, the elasticity of supply is given by:

4.2 $\eta = |[(Q_{S2} - Q_{S1})/\{(Q_{S1} + Q_{S2})/2\}] \div [(P_2 - P_1)/\{(P_1 + P_2)/2\}]|$

where "η" (the Greek letter eta) will be our symbol for the elasticity of supply. Notice, that with the elasticity of supply, η would normally be calculated as a positive number even without the absolute value sign. However, it makes elasticity easier to calculate and remember the equation if we use the same equation for elasticity of supply and demand. This also helps to make it easier to interpret the values for elasticity of supply and demand.

The table below outlines the terms we use to characterize the elasticities of supply and demand:

TABLE 4.1

Value of ε, η	Characterization of Elasticity
$\varepsilon, \eta = 0$	Perfectly Inelastic
$0 < \varepsilon, \eta < 1$	Inelastic
$\varepsilon, \eta = 1$	Unit Elastic
$1 < \varepsilon, \eta < \infty$	Elastic
$\varepsilon, \eta = \infty$	Perfectly Elastic

There are several factors that affect the elasticity of either supply or demand. We will discuss first the factors affecting the elasticity of demand. One factor that affects the elasticity of demand is the degree to which a good is a necessity or a luxury. Goods that are necessities will tend to be more inelastic, whereas luxuries will tend to be more elastic.

A second factor that will affect the elasticity of demand is whether you are measuring the short-term or more longer-term responsiveness of demand to a change in price. In the short term, it is more difficult for individuals to alter their patterns of behavior, but in the longer term individuals can change their behavior in response to price changes.

A third factor that may affect the elasticity of demand is the availability of substitutes. Goods for which there is no close substitute will tend to exhibit greater inelasticity of demand than goods that have easily available substitutes.

A fourth factor that may affect the elasticity of demand for an item is whether the item is a "big ticket" item or not. The elasticity of demand for eggs may be low because they are relatively inexpensive; a price increase may not be significant enough to induce changes in egg consumption whereas a change in the price of cars might have a more significant impact on the quantity demanded for cars.

We will not go into as much detail on the factors affecting the elasticity of supply. In general, technical factors and the industry structure will have the most impact on the elasticity of supply. These tend to be topics that are more central to microeconomic analysis and thus, we won't focus on this here to a great extent. Two factors that would affect the elasticity of supply would be the flexibility of the production process – elasticity of supply would tend to be greater the more there are different techniques or processes for making the same good — and the number of different producers – if there is only one producer in an industry that would tend to lead to lower elasticity of supply and vice versa.

There are other types of elasticities of demand that can be calculated. The cross price elasticity of demand relates to the percentage change in the quantity demanded for a good for a change in the price of another good. If goods are substitutes or complements a change in the price of the related good could lead to an impact on the quantity demanded for a good. However, again, this is more of a microeconomics topic and we will not focus on this here.

Another type of elasticity that is worth discussing here is the "income elasticity of demand." The income elasticity of demand is the percentage change in the quantity demanded for a good for a percentage change in income. "Normal goods" have positive values when calculating the income elasticity of demand; "inferior goods" have negative values for the income elasticity of demand. Mathematically, we calculate the income elasticity of demand as follows:

4.3 Income elasticity of demand =

$$[(Q_{D2} - Q_{D1})/\{(Q_{D1} + Q_{D2})/2\}] \div [(Y_2 - Y_1)/\{(Y_1 + Y_2)/2\}]$$

It is important to note that elasticities of supply and demand are not the same thing as slopes of supply and demand functions. In fact elasticity can change even along linear demand and supply curves. Let's look at an example.

Table 4.2

The Demand and Supply Schedules for Oil

Price (per barrel)	Q_D (millions of barrels)	Q_S (millions of barrels)
$100	55	92.5
$90	60	90
$80	65	87.5
$70	70	85
$60	75	82.5
$50	80	80
$40	85	77.5
$30	90	75
$20	95	72.5
$10	100	70

Figure 4.1
The Supply and Demand for Oil

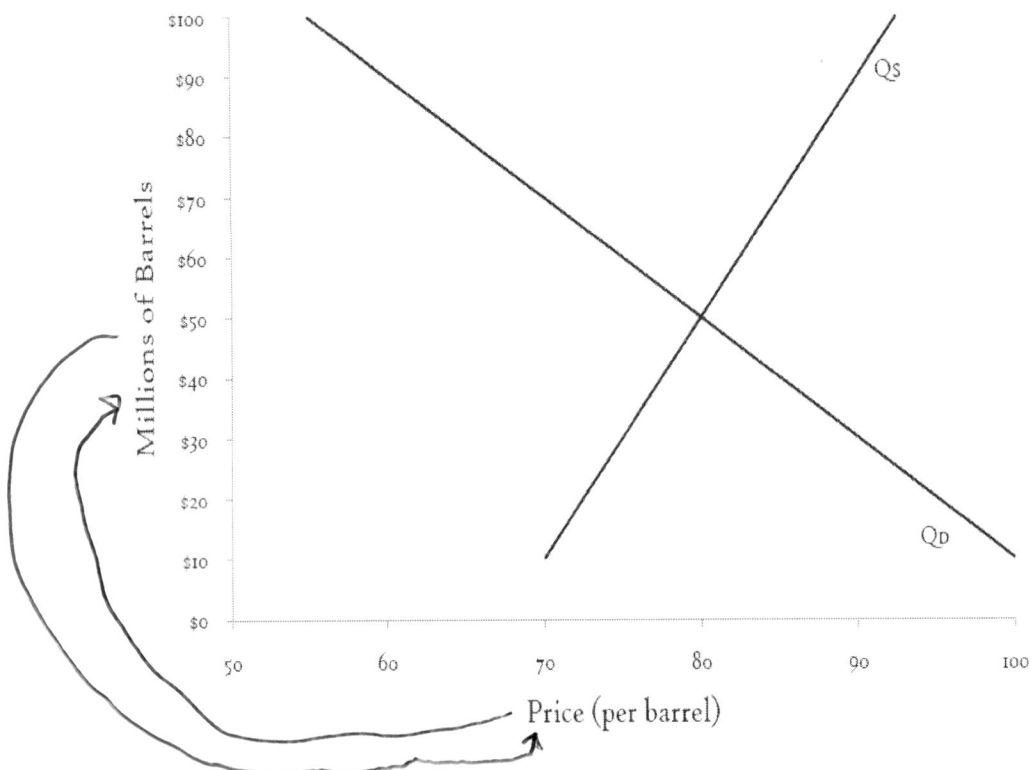

Notice that the supply and demand for oil are in *equilibrium* when the price per barrel equals 50. Supply equals demand at 80 million barrels of oil. Let's calculate the elasticity of demand and the elasticity of supply using the midpoint method between a price of $40 and $60. We find an elasticity of demand of 0.3125 and an elasticity of supply of 0.15625. We would characterize both of these elasticities as inelastic, with supply being even more inelastic since the magnitude of the elasticity is smaller for supply.

Try and calculate the elasticities of supply and demand at other points along the demand and supply schedules. You should get different values than those calculated above even though the supply and demand schedules are linear. Just remember, elasticity is not the same concept as slope and we generally cannot guess the elasticities of supply and demand just by looking at a graph or by calculating the slope. Only when the demand or supply curves are perfectly horizontal or vertical will we be able to determine the elasticities visually. This will be the case only when the demand or supply curve is perfectly elastic or inelastic.

Practice Problems for Chapter 4

1. Given the following supply and demand schedules for car washing services in the United States

P	Q_d	Q_s
	(millions of washes per week)	(millions of washes per week)
20	10	40
18	20	35
16	30	30
14	40	25
12	50	20
10	60	15

a) Calculate the elasticities of supply and demand at the equilibrium price and quantity. (Hint: use the values for Q_d and Q_s when the price changes from one increment above the equilibrium price to one increment below.)

b) Characterize the elasticities of demand and supply at this point (e.g., elastic, inelastic, etc.)

c) If there is an increase in supply for some reason, would you expect total revenue (P x Q) to go up or down? Explain.

4.6

Chapter 5

Consumer Choice under Conditions of Scarcity

In this chapter we begin to develop a theory of the consumer. In particular, we wish to build the basic model of how consumers make decisions under conditions of scarcity. If all goods were produced in abundance, there would be no need for this type of theory. However, we know that most people do not have unlimited resources and therefore economists have motivation for developing a theory of the consumer constrained to make decisions when there are limits on their consumption possibilities. We start with the question of how consumers form preferences and try to see if we can establish some patterns or conditions for those preferences.

Economists have invented the concept of *utility* to mean the well-being or level of satisfaction of the consumer. We start with the assumption that the goal for consumers is to maximize utility. This makes intuitive sense as it is not hard to accept that most rational people try to increase their sense of well-being, although this may mean different things to different people. A well-crafted theory of the consumer should allow for people to have different preferences as we all know this to be true in reality.

To make our theory of the consumer workable, we need to formulate some basic assumptions about consumer behavior and incorporate this into our theory. We start with three basic assumptions:

1) Consumers are able to rank their preferences.
2) More of a good is always better.
3) Preferences are transitive or consistent with each other

Consumers are able to rank their preferences

This does not mean that there can't be ties in preferences—consumers might be "indifferent" between one bundle of goods and another bundle of different goods—but it does mean that consumers know themselves and are able to rank all of their preferences. By assuming this, we don't allow consumers to say "I don't know" when we ask them to rank their preferences. When comparing bundles of goods, either one bundle will be preferred to the other, the consumer will be indifferent between the two bundles, or the other bundle will be preferred.

More of a good is always better

Although it is often true that as we consume more and more of an item we sometimes get tired of it, we will presume here that more of a good is always better. Since consumers are constrained from consuming everything they might desire, usually consumers will be choosing allocations of goods such that even the last unit or a good consumed still provides some increment to utility. Another way of saying this is the "marginal utility"—the change in utility for a change in the consumption of a good-- is always greater than zero. Thus, more of a good will always be better.

Preferences are transitive

If a consumer prefers consumption bundle A to consumption bundl/e B, and consumption bundle B to consumption bundle C, by transitivity, that same consumer must prefer consumption bundle A to consumption bundle C. What we are really saying here is nothing more than preferences should be consistent.

The Consumer's Indifference Curves

As we build our model of the consumer, an important building block is the concept of *indifference curves*. Indifference curves are curves in a graph along which utility is held constant. For example, in Figure 5.1 below, I_0, I_1, and I_2 represent three different indifference curves. The indifference curves represent bundles of goods A and B such that each bundle gives the consumer the exact same level of utility. As the consumer moves from I_0 to I_1 to I_2, the consumer is able to achieve higher levels of utility. We will see later that a consumer will always prefer to consume at the highest possible indifference curve where he/she can reach the highest level of utility, subject to his/her ability to afford a particular consumption bundle.

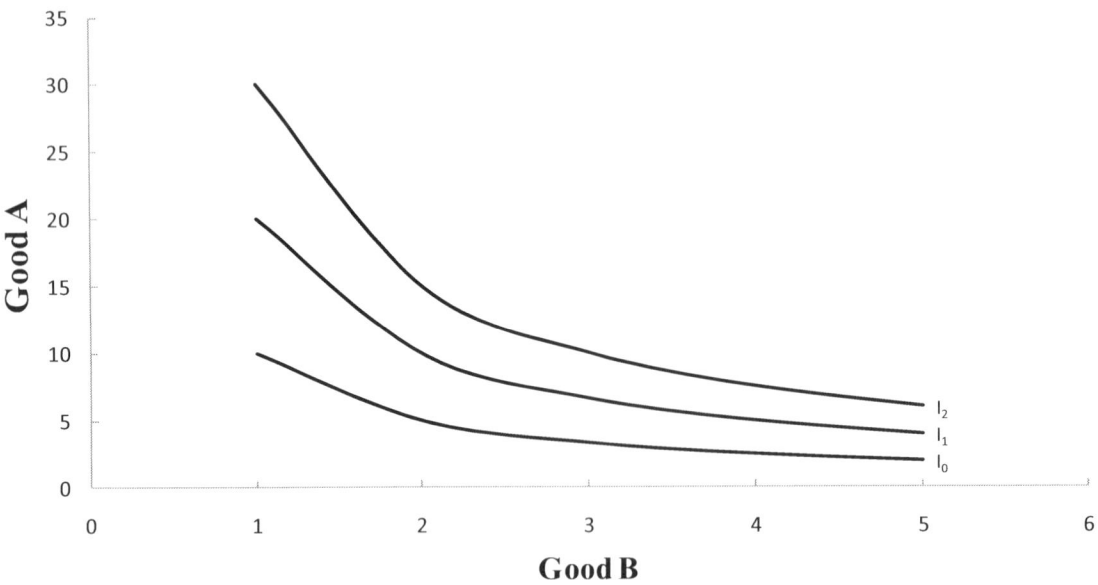

**Figure 5.1
A Consumer's Indifference Curves**

In the graph above, we see indifference curves whose shape we will describe as "convex to the origin." Indifference curves do not always have to have this shape, but this will be the most common shape. With indifference curves that have this shape, a consumer gets "diminishing marginal utility" from consuming more and more of an item. While holding utility constant along an indifference curve, a consumer will have to be enticed with greater and greater amounts of Good A to be willing to give up successive increments of Good B, because of this characteristic of diminishing marginal utility.

Since utility is constant along an indifference curve, it must be true that for any increase in good A, the extra utility that is gained by that change will be exactly offset by a decrease in utility coming from good B to hold utility constant. The slope of the indifference curve reflects the rate at which the individual will exchange one good for another holding utility constant. Economists have a name for this slope: the ***marginal rate of substitution* (MRS)**. The name comes from the idea that in order to give up an increment of utility from a small decrease in the consumption of a good, the consumer must be compensated (or substituted) with an increase in utility from the other good. This is an important idea and we will use this later in the chapter to find the consumer's optimum level of consumption.

Indifference curves cannot have any of the following characteristics:

1) Indifference curves cannot be "fat" or more than one point in width. (This would violate the "more is better" assumption.)

2) Indifference curves cannot cross. (This would violate the transitivity assumption as well as "more is better".)
3) Indifference curves cannot have a positive slope. (Again, this would violate the more is better idea.)

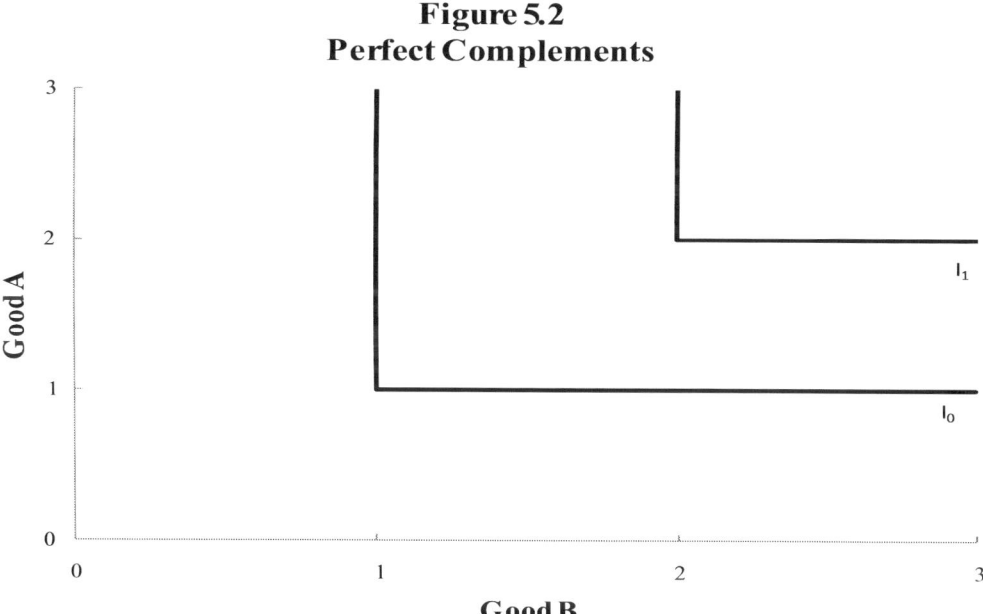

**Figure 5.2
Perfect Complements**

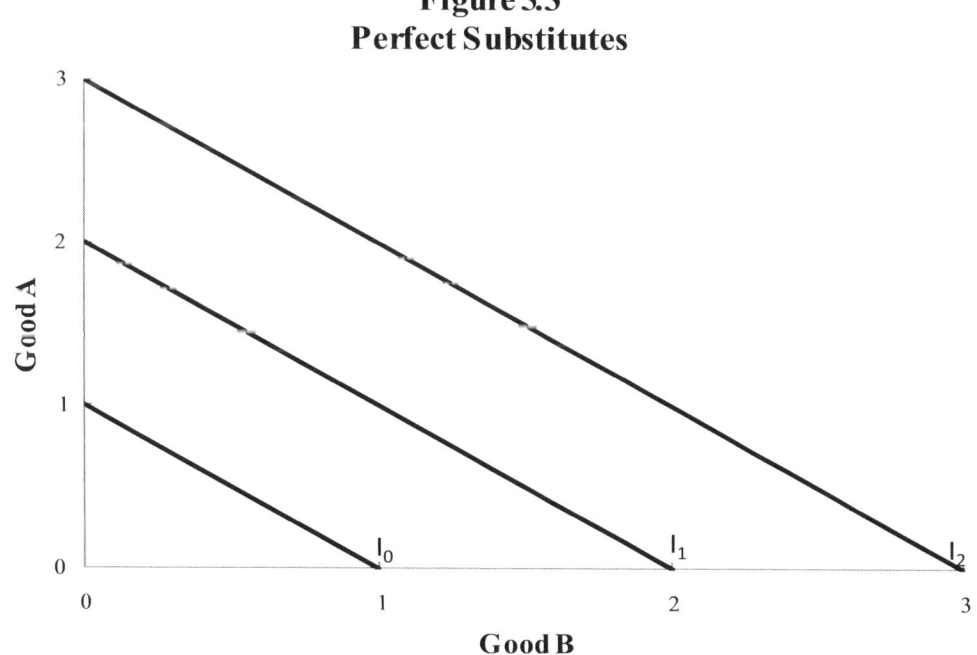

**Figure 5.3
Perfect Substitutes**

Figures 5.2 and 5.3 illustrate the extremes in the shapes that indifference curves might have. Figure 5.2 illustrates the case of "perfect complements". These are goods that the consumer prefers to consume in fixed proportions. Consider the case of an individual who likes to eat ice cream in a cone. In this case, the consumer will need one cone for each scoop of ice cream. To get to a higher level of utility, he/she will need to be able to purchase both the additional scoop of ice cream and the additional cone. Figure 5.3 illustrates the case of "perfect substitutes." In this case, the two goods are perfectly substitutable—the consumer is indifferent between consuming Good A or Good B and will exchange one good for the other at a fixed rate. An example might be two different brands of the same type of soft drink; some people may not have any preference between the two brands. As long as they are the same price, one will be exchanged for the other without changing utility.

The Utility Function

Although most of us probably aren't aware that we have one, economists posit the idea that individuals have a utility function. This is simply the idea that there is a mathematical relationship between the things that give us pleasure or utility and the level of utility itself. In many ways, a utility function is analogous to a production function for the firm. The firm takes inputs to the production process (capital, labor, etc.) and gets output. The individual consumes a basket of goods, producing a certain level of utility for the consumer.

Let's start with a very simple utility function with only one good:

5.1 $U = f(A)$

This says simply that utility is a function of good A. Graphically, this might be represented as:

Figure 5.4

A Simple Utility Function

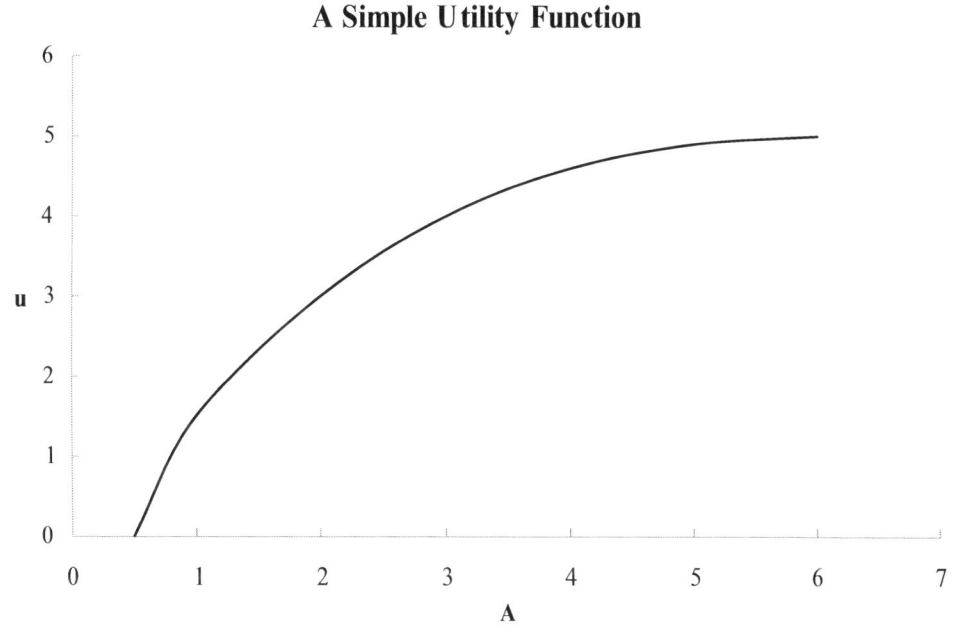

Marginal Utility of A

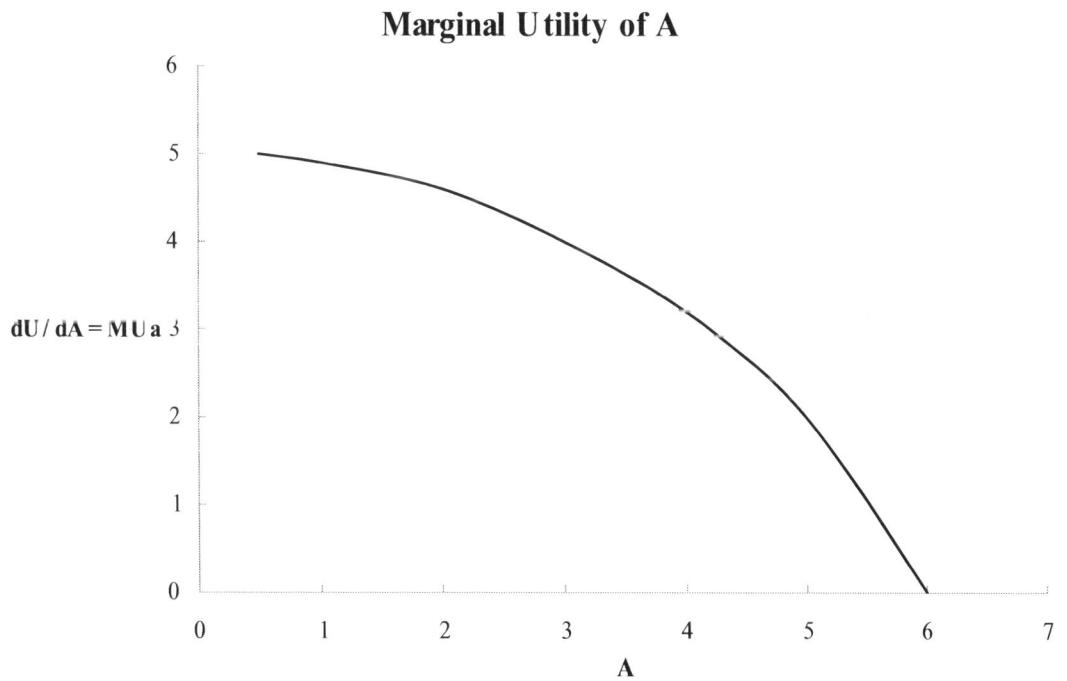

The lower graph in Figure 5.4 represents the "marginal utility of A". This is the incremental change in utility for an incremental change in the quantity of A consumed. Using calculus, this would be the derivative of utility with respect to A or dU/dA. Without using calculus, the marginal utility of A can be represented as $\Delta U/\Delta A$. where "Δ" is the Greek letter delta and it represents change or difference of a variable, or in this case, the change in utility for a change in A.

Notice that the marginal of utility of A approaches zero, but never becomes negative. Although the consumer gets diminishing marginal utility from A as the consumption of A increases, because of the more is better rule it cannot become negative.

The Budget Constraint for the Consumer

To make things relatively simple, let's suppose a consumer allocates $100 per month for expenditures on entertainment. As entertainment, this individual either goes to the movies, which costs $10, or goes out to dinner, which costs $20. Letting M equal the number of movies attended per month and D equal to the number of dinners out per month, we can describe the consumer's budget constraint as follows:

4.4 $Y = P_M \times M + P_D \times D$

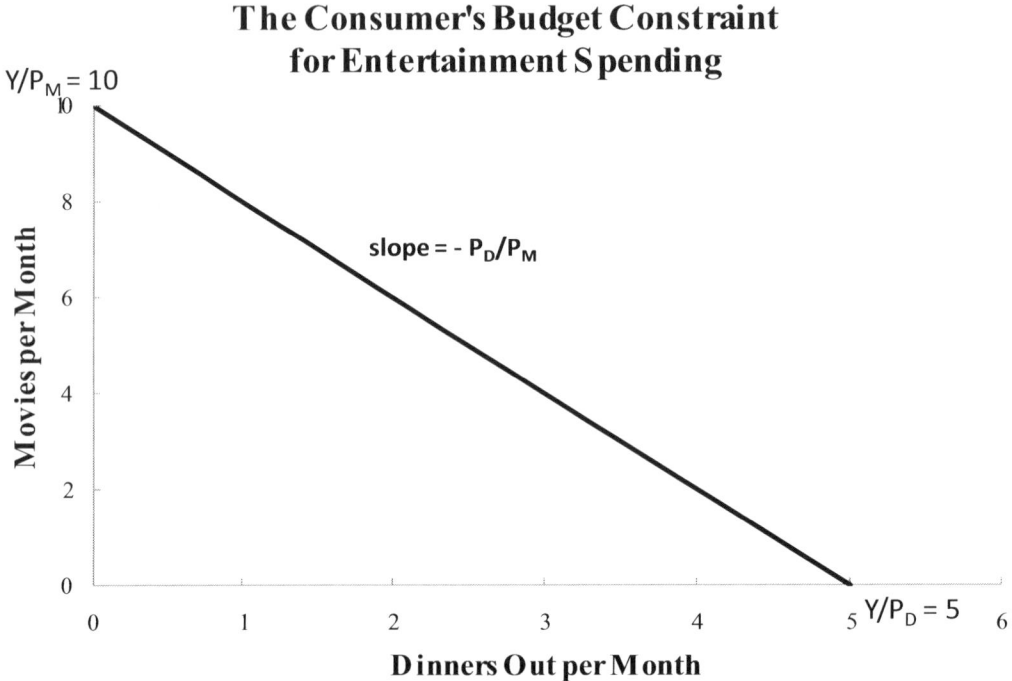

Figure 5.5
The Consumer's Budget Constraint for Entertainment Spending

Where Y represents the monthly budget, P_M is the price of a movie, and P_D is the price of a dinner out. Substituting in the values given above, we get $100 = 10M + 20D$. This is the budget constraint for the consumer. This is an equation in two variables, which turns out to be a straight line, and is graphed in Figure 5.5 above.

The intercepts are found by taking Y divided by the price of each good. We can calculate the slope by taking the rise over the run, which equals $(Y/P_M) / -(Y/P_D) = -(P_D/P_M)$. This slope of the budget constraint also has a name: the ***marginal rate of transformation* (MRT)**.

Finding the Consumer's Optimum

The goal of each consumer is to maximize utility subject to his/her budget constraint. When the consumer has convex to the origin indifference curves, if there is a point of tangency between an indifference curve and the budget constrain, that must be the optimum for the consumer. Remember, the consumer prefers to be on the highest possible indifference curve, meaning furthest from the origin in a "northeast" direction (up and to the right). If there is a unique point of tangency, that's the highest possible indifference curve. If this point of tangency exists, the marginal rate of substitution is equal to the marginal rate of transformation at that point. The slope of the consumer's indifference curve is equal to the slope of the budget constraint at the point of tangency.

Practice Problems for Chapter 5

1. Suppose a college sports fan budgets $60 per month for tickets to basketball and hockey games. The hockey tickets cost $5 each and the basketball tickets cost $10. Draw a simple graph for the consumer's budget constraint.
   a) Calculate the marginal rate of transformation.
   b) What condition must be satisfied if there is a unique point of tangency?

2. Explain why indifference curves can't cross. Explain why they can't be positively sloped.

3. A consumer enjoys eating vanilla ice cream with chocolate sauce. Suppose that the price of a gallon of ice cream is $4 and the price of a pint of chocolate sauce is $2. Suppose the consumer allocates $24 per month for expenditures on ice cream and chocolate sauce. Suppose also that the consumer always consumes exactly one pint of chocolate sauce for each gallon of ice cream consumed. Draw the consumer's budget constraint and find the consumer's optimum. What do the consumer's indifference curve look like if the consumer always consumes the ice cream and chocolate sauce in fixed proportions? Is there a unique point of tangency? How do we know how to find the optimum?

Chapter 6

Consumer Surplus, Producer Surplus and Welfare Analysis

Suppose you could survey individuals and ask them the maximum price they would be willing to pay for a cup of premium coffee. Assuming they could be persuaded to be completely honest with you, you might be able to get them to tell you how much they would be willing to pay to buy two, three or more cups of premium coffee per month. Now, if you were the owner of a coffee shop, you might be able to attempt to charge your customers the exact maximum price they would be willing to pay to buy coffee. However, after a while, your customers would probably catch on to your game and start to "lowball" your surveys.

So in practice, it is very difficult to charge each customer for a particular good the exact maximum price the customer would be willing to pay. Most customers are able to buy goods below their maximum *reservation price*—the maximum price they would be willing to pay. We call the difference between what customers would be willing to pay for a good and the amount they actually pay for a good, their *consumer surplus*.

In Figure 6.1 below, the market price for a cup of premium coffee is $3.00. The area below the demand curve and above the price represents consumer surplus—the well-being that is derived by consumers because they are able to buy premium coffee below their reservation price, or the price that they would have been willing to pay.

**Figure 6.1
Consumer and Producer Surplus
in the Premium Coffee Market**

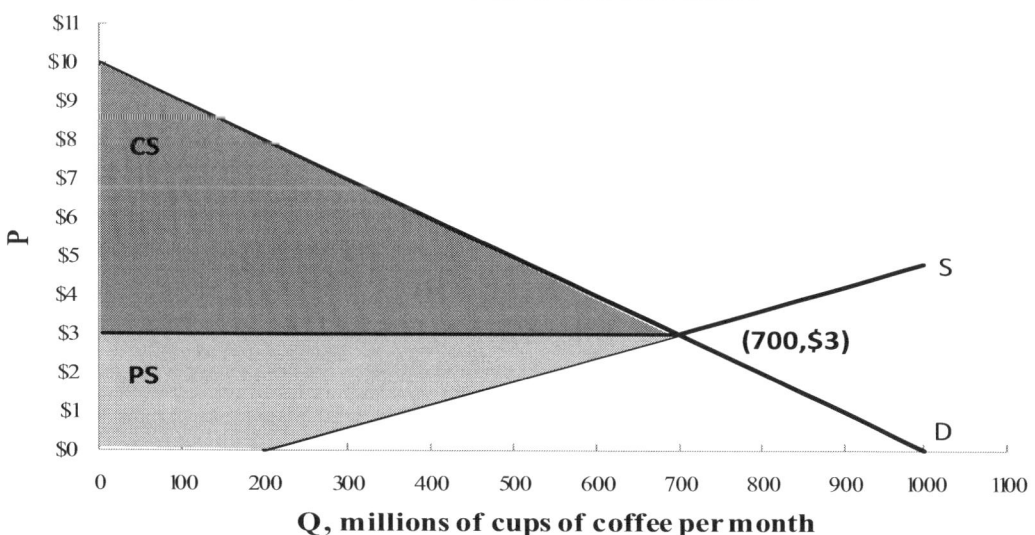

The area of consumer surplus could be calculated mathematically, if we knew the equations for the demand curve and the supply curve. Here will focus on the geometric area as our measure of consumer surplus.

Producer surplus is similarly defined as the difference between the price at which producers would be willing to supply their goods and the price received in the marketplace for their goods. Thus in Figure 6.1, producer surplus is the area above the supply curve and below the price.

We define **welfare** as the sum of consumer surplus plus producer surplus. Welfare here indicates only the total surplus that is available given market conditions; it does not have anything to say about how equitable the distribution of that surplus is to market participants. Thus, it could be possible in some circumstances that consumers get all the surplus and in others that producers get all the surplus. We will not adjust welfare to compensate for imbalances in the distribution of the surplus in any way. Thus, the welfare analysis we are undertaking here is really a measure of **efficiency** and not **equity**. Later, we will add to our definition of welfare by adding any government revenues and subtracting any government expense. As long as some party, either the consumer, the producer, or the government, is getting some surplus, we wish to count it in our measure of welfare.

Suppose there is a technological innovation that makes it cheaper to produce coffee and this results in a rightward shift of the supply curve by 50 (million).

The new equilibrium in the coffee market is shown in Figure 6.2 on the next page.

**Figure 6.2
The New Equilibrium in the Market for Premium Coffee**

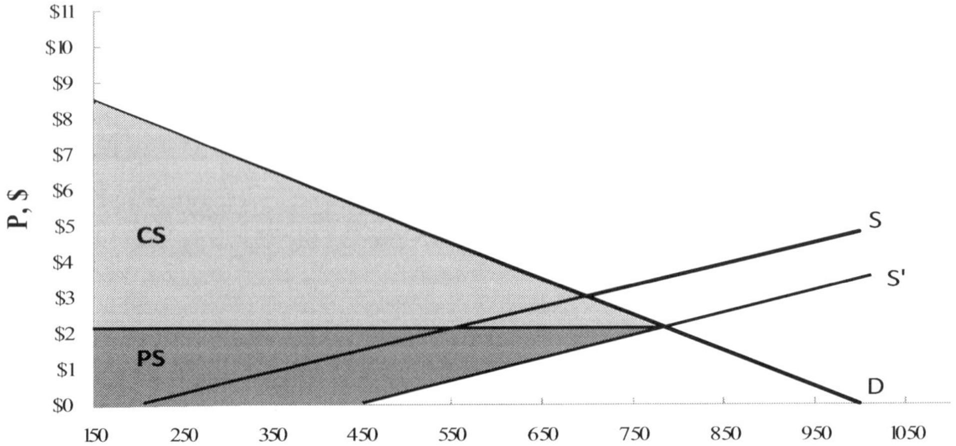

The shift in supply leads to rises in consumer surplus, producer surplus and welfare.

In Figure 6.3 below, we look at the effects on welfare where a producer is compelled to produce above the competitive equilibrium level of output. In the matrix below the graph, we outline the (1) Competitive Equilibrium, (2) Larger Output, and (3) the change or Δ, which is column (2) minus column (1). We will generally follow this technique of analysis when we perform these welfare calculations and something has changed in our graph. Note that when a change in welfare is negative, we call this a **deadweight loss**. When the change in welfare is positive, it would be called a **deadweight gain**.

Figure 6.3
Forcing a Producer to Produce Above the Competitive Equilibrium Lowers Welfare

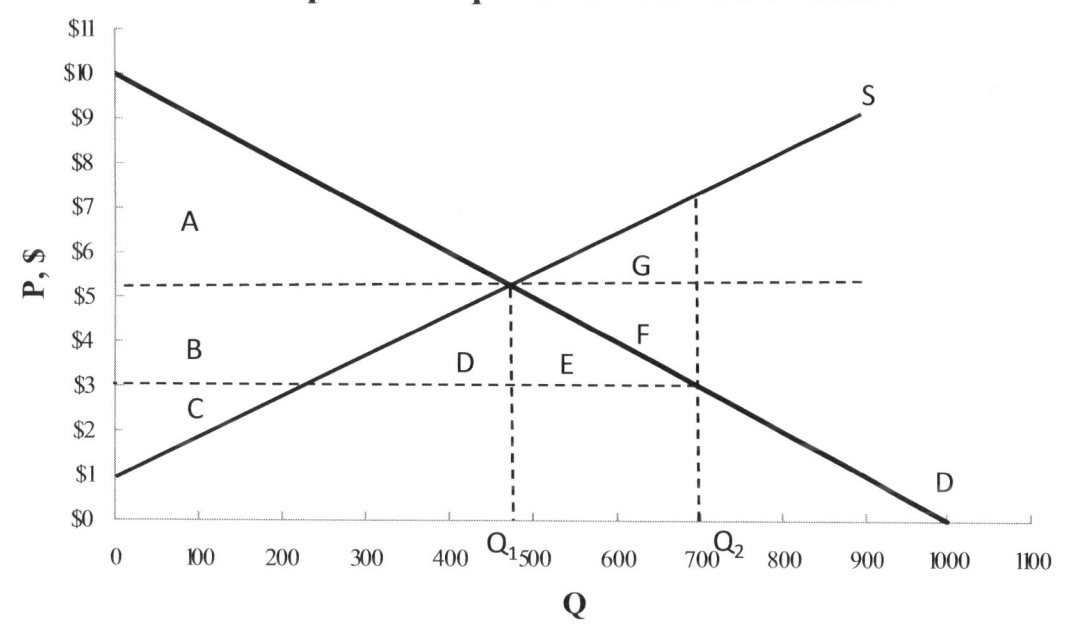

	(1) Competitive Equilibrium	(2) Higher Output	(2 – 1) Δ (change)
Consumer Surplus	A	A + B + D + E	B + D + E
Producer Surplus	B + C	C – D – E – F – G	– B – D – E – F – G
Welfare	A + B + C	A + B + C – F – G	– F – G = DWL

In Figure 6.4, we analyze the effects on welfare when a producer is forced to produce less than the competitive level of output. This also leads to a deadweight loss. Most of the time, producing at the competitive equilibrium is the most efficient solution in terms of welfare analysis, as we shall see.

Figure 6.4
Forcing a Producer to Produce Less Than the Competitive Equilibrium Lowers Welfare

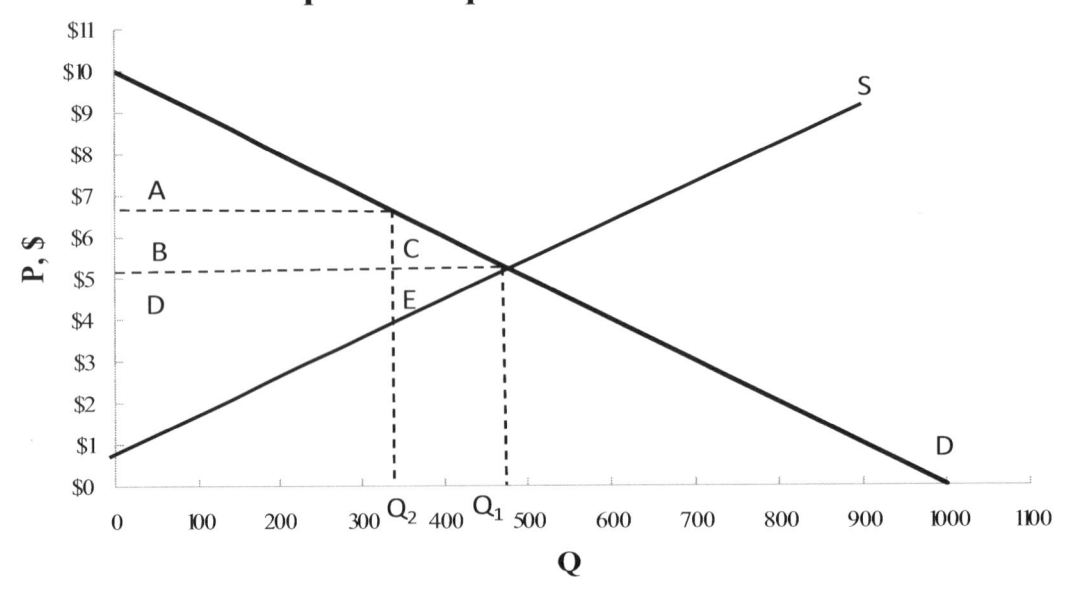

	(1) Competitive Equilibrium	(2) Lower Output	(2 – 1) Δ (change)
Consumer Surplus	A + B + C	A	- B - C
Producer Surplus	D + E	B + D	B - E
Welfare	A + B + C + D + E	A + B + D	- C – E = DWL

In Figure 6.5, we explore the effects of a per unit tax (specific tax) on chocolate candies. In this instance, the government authorities collect the tax, so we have to add in government revenues (T = τ Q) when calculating welfare and changes in welfare. Again, we are deviating from the competitive equilibrium and this leads to a decline in welfare and a deadweight loss (= - D – G - I).

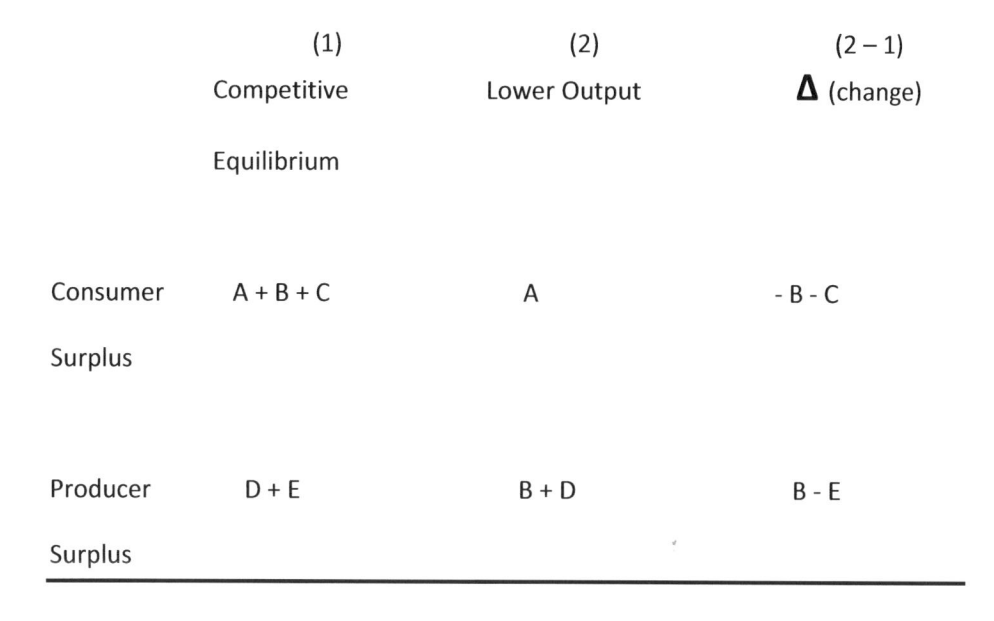

Figure 6.5
A Per-Unit or Specific Tax on Chocolate Candies Paid by Producer

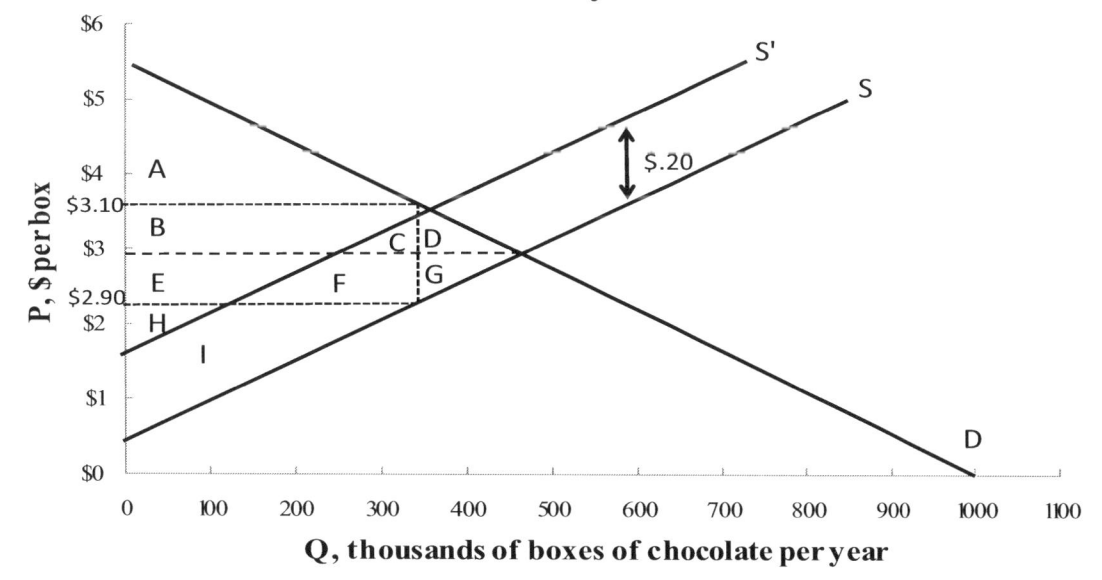

	(1) Competitive Equilibrium	(2) With Specific Tax	(2 – 1) Δ (change)
Consumer Surplus	A + B + C + D	A	- B – C – D
Producer Surplus	E + F + G + H + I	H	-E – F – G - I
Government Revenue	0	B + C + E + F	B + C + E + F
Welfare	A + B + C + D + E + F + G + H + I	A + H + B + C + E + F	- D – G – I = DWL

Practice Problems for Chapter 6

1. Under what conditions do you think welfare analysis for a government program would tend to lead to a deadweight gain?

2. Try to draw the graphs for forcing a producer to produce: 1) above the competitive equilibrium level of output and 2) below the competitive equilibrium level of output. Try to draw the matrix for consumer surplus, producer surplus and welfare for the initial situation, the changed situation and calculate the change. Is there a deadweight loss?

3. Try to draw the graph before and after a specific tax and draw the matrix for consumer surplus, producer surplus, government revenue and welfare for the initial situation, with the tax and for the change. Find the area of the deadweight loss.

Chapter 7

Income and Substitution Effects and Consumer Choice

Let's look at how a consumer's consumption choices change in response to price changes. We start with a consumer who allocates a certain proportion of his monthly income for soft drink purchases. This person either purchases lemon-lime drinks or cola drinks. How will his choices change as the price of one type of soda changes relative to the other?

In the top part of Figure 7.1 below, we see a curve that represents the consumption choices of the consumer as the price of cola changes. The curve is mapped out by the tangents of his indifference curves to the different budget constraints as the price of cola varies. The swinging to the right of the budget constraint represents a falling of the price of cola drinks.

Figure 7.1
Derivation of an Individual's Demand Curve

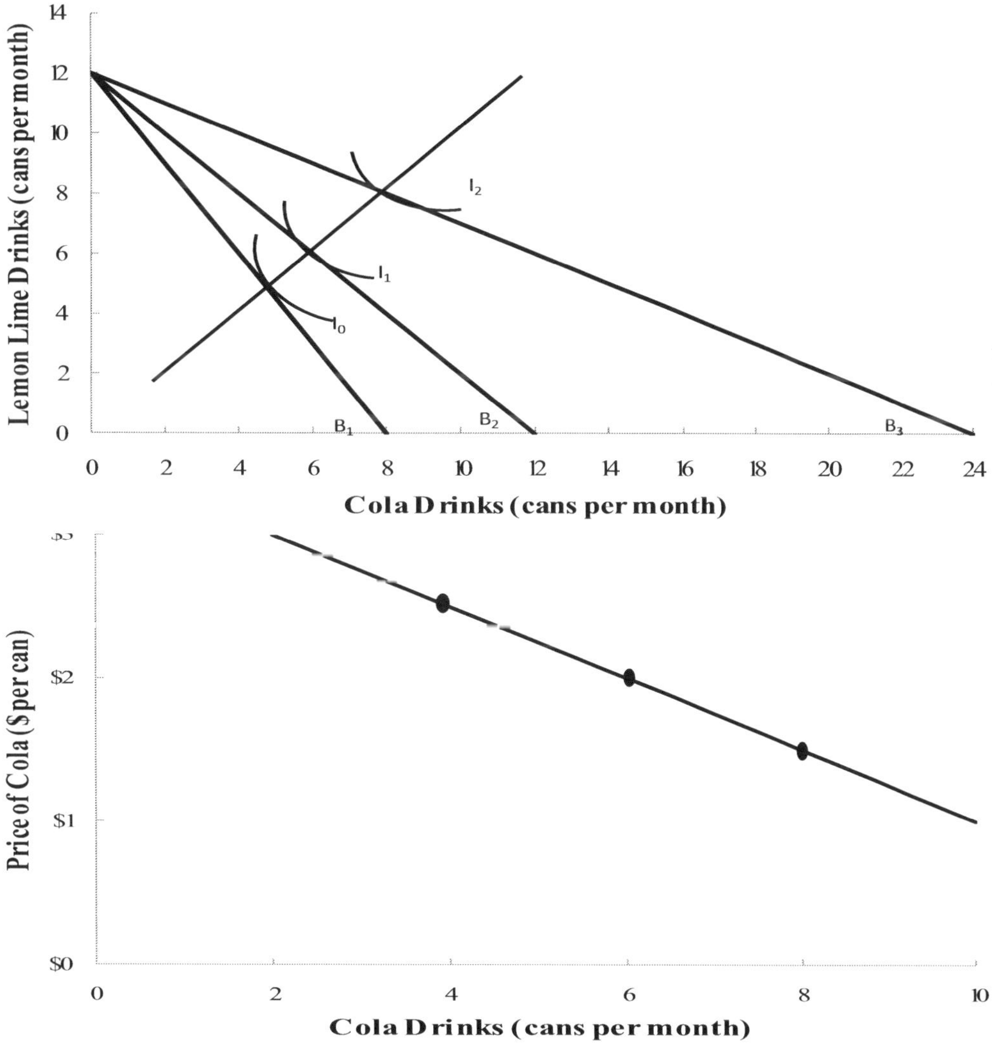

In the bottom part of the figure, the price of cola drinks is mapped against the individual's consumption choices. The end result is the individual's demand curve for cola.

Next, let's look at how an individual's consumption choices change when income changes. The ***Engel curve*** maps out how an individual's consumption of a commodity changes as income changes.

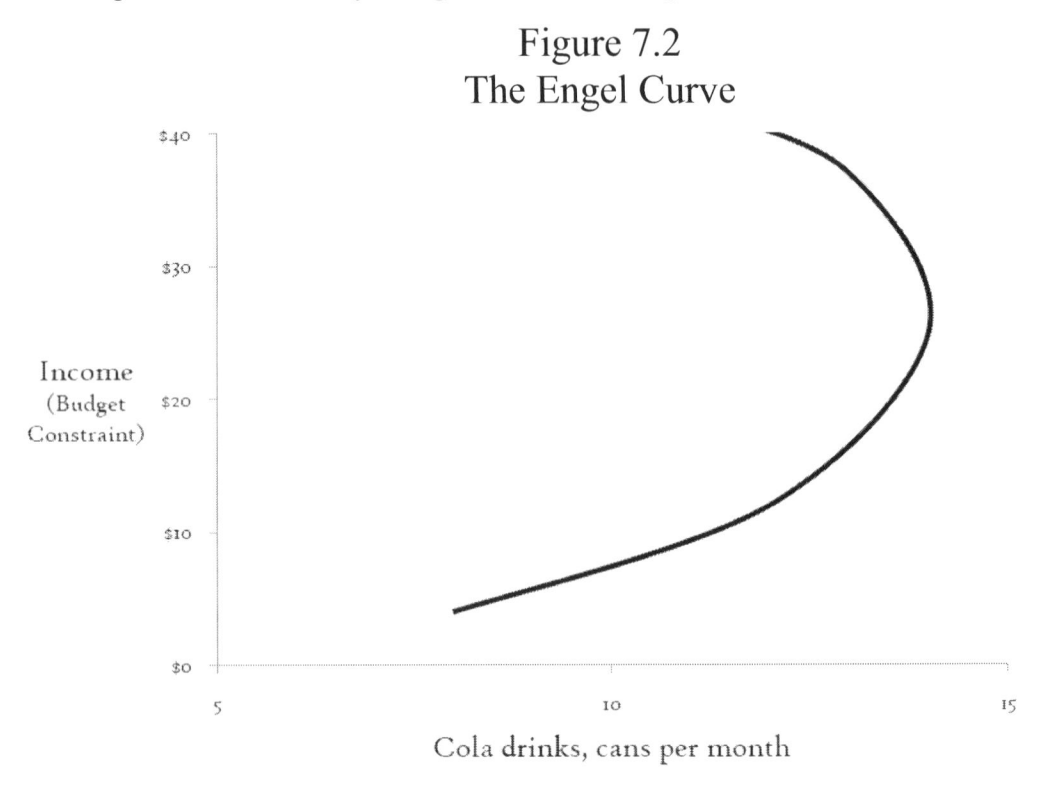

Figure 7.2
The Engel Curve

Cola drinks, cans per month

Note that the curve is at first positively slopes but later becomes negatively sloped. For this consumer, cola is a normal good at low levels of income and an inferior good at higher levels of income.

In Figure 7.3, we look at how the consumer optimizes between two goods as income changes. We can see once again that both goods, steak and pizza, are normal at low levels of income, but as income increases, pizza becomes an inferior good because consumption of pizza goes down as income continues to increase.

Figure 7.3
Consumer Optimization as Income Changes

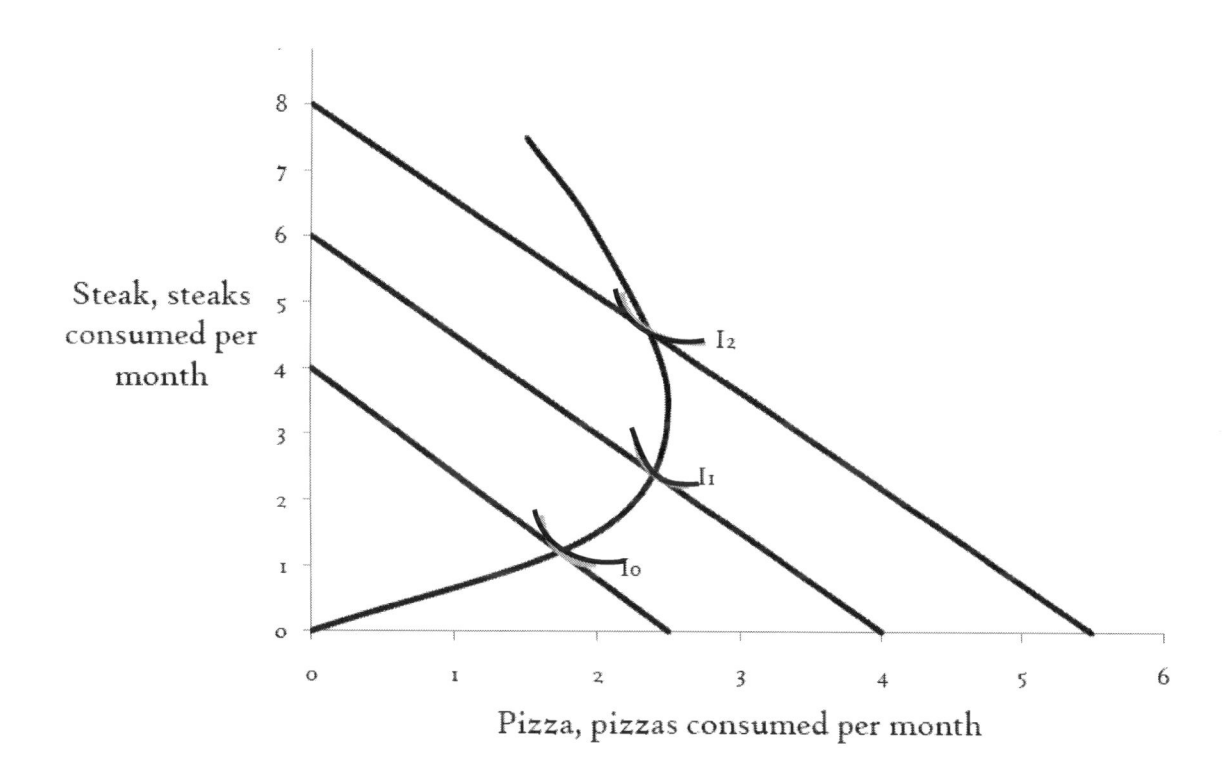

Steak, steaks consumed per month (y-axis)

Pizza, pizzas consumed per month (x-axis)

Income and Substitution Effects

This brings us to two very important concepts in economics: ***income*** and ***substitution effects***. Note that when the price changes for a commodity, holding all else constant, two things will happen as a result.

1) the relative price of that good will change relative to all other goods, and
2) the consumer, assuming he purchases at least some of the good, will be made either poorer or richer because of the price change.

Thus, when analyzing the consumer's choice in response to a relative price change for a good, we can break down the impact into these two effects: the substitution effect and the income effect.

Figure 7.4
Income and Substitution Effects

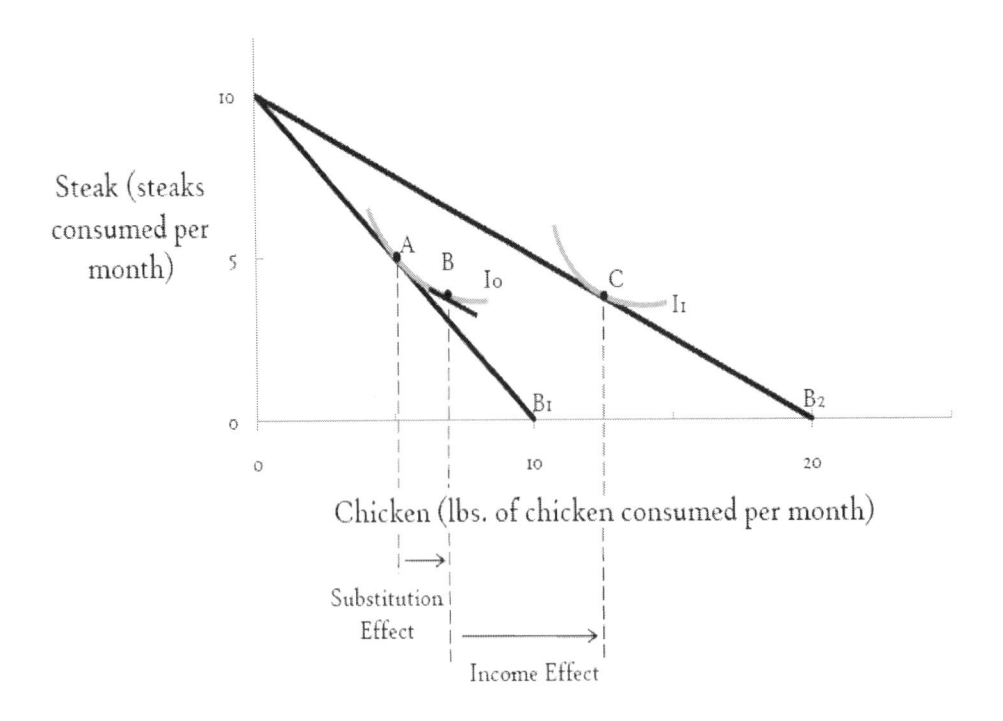

In Figure 7.4 above, the price of chicken is dropping in half from budget constraint L_1 to budget constraint L_2. We break down the change in the consumption bundle into two components. First, we look at the change from the relative price change, holding utility constant. To do this, we draw a line parallel to the new budget constraint—to mimic the relative price change—and tangent to the initial indifference curve. In Figure 7.4, this is the move from A to B. This component of the change in the consumption of chicken is called the "substitution effect". As the price changes to make chicken relatively less expensive, *ceteris paribus*, the consumer will substitute chicken for steak.

The rest of the change for the consumer, from B to C, is called the "income effect." The only thing changing from B to C is the income level of the consumer. The relative prices of chicken and steak are constant as we move from B to C. Only income is changing, hence the term income effect.

The Case of a Giffen Good

Most of the time when the price of a good or commodity declines, consumers will tend to increase their consumption of that good. However, there may be instances where this tendency does not hold. We illustrate in Figure 7.5 below, the case of a **Giffen good**. This is a good that a consumer will consume less of as its price goes down.

Figure 7.5
Rice as a Giffen Good

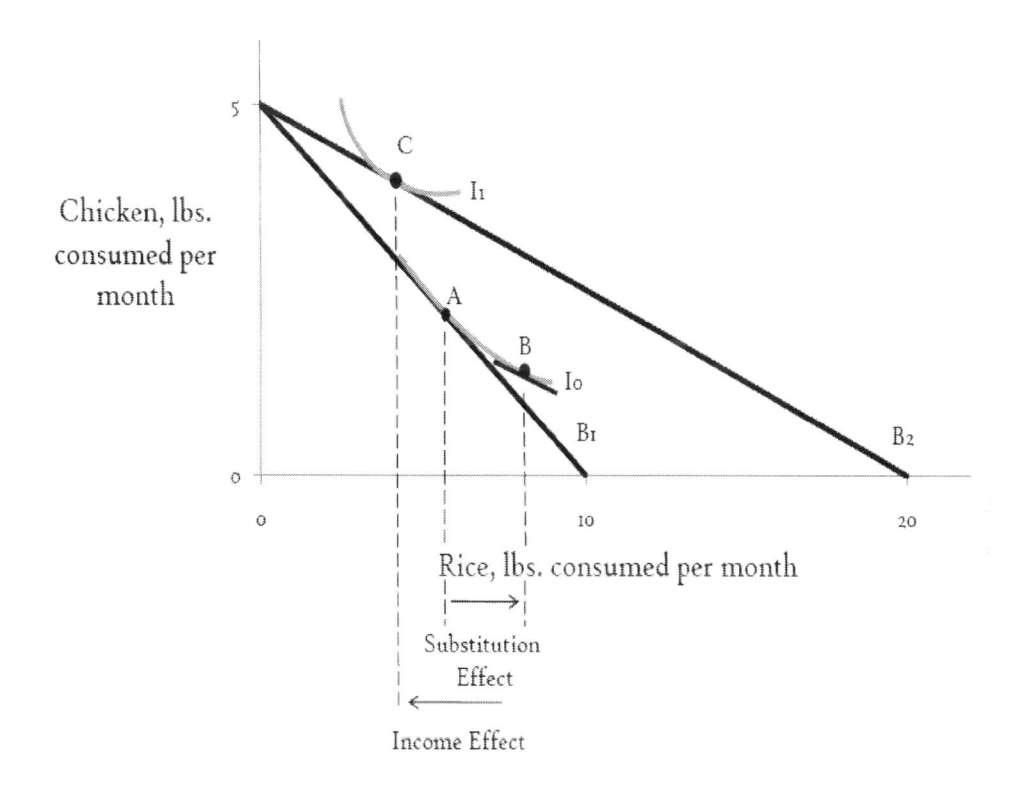

Consider the case of a relatively poor person who consumes two basic goods: chicken and rice. Since rice is cheaper, the individual may consume a lot of rice as her basic sustenance. Suppose the price of rice goes down as in Figure 7.5 moving from budget constraint L_1 to L_2. The substitution effect goes in the normal direction—toward greater consumption of rice. However, for this consumer rice is an inferior good, so the income effect as rice comes down in price is toward the greater consumption of chicken. In the case of a Giffen good, the substitution and income effects go in opposite directions, but the income effect is bigger in magnitude than the substitution effect. For this person, rice is such a staple of her consumption that the positive effect of a drop in its price on alleviating the budget constraint, allows her to stop consuming so much rice and increase her consumption of the relative luxury good, chicken. Thus, the price of rice drops, but she ends up consuming less of it!

The Labor/Leisure Decision

It turns out that we can apply some of the same "technology" or tools of analysis we have been developing here to analyze the "labor/leisure" decision. Individuals have to choose how much time their going to spend working and we'll assume the rest of the time, other than sleeping, that they're at leisure. These choices will be affected by the return individuals receive for work—the *wage*—and will also have an income and substitution effect as in the goods problems we have been discussing.

Let's define **z** as the number of hours of work per day and let's assume the most an individual can work per day on a regular basis is 16 hours. (We'll leave 8 hours for sleep.) If **x** is the number of hours of leisure per day, then **x + z = 16**, or **x = 16 – z**.

We illustrate the labor/leisure decision in Figure 7.6

Figure 7.6
The Labor/Leisure Decision

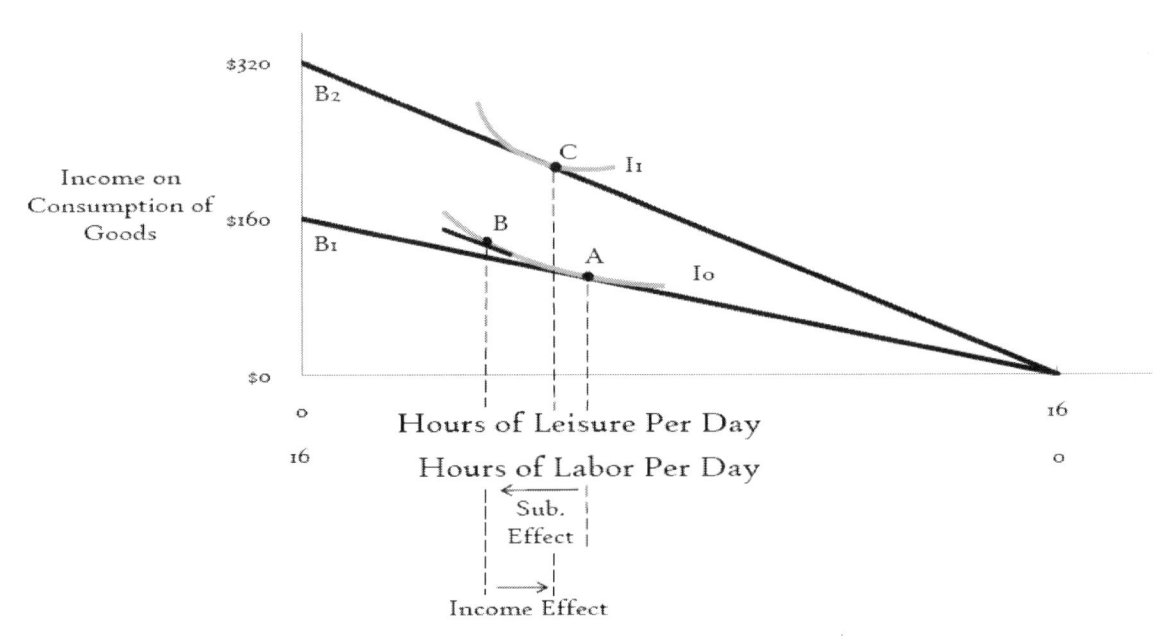

7.6

L_1 represents the original budget constraint of sorts. Consumption possibilities are determined by how many hours the individual works. The individual here chooses between consumption of goods or consumption of leisure. The wage rate along L_1 is $10 per hour. If the individual works the maximum 16 hours per day, he earns $160. If the wage doubles, the budget constraint shifts up to L_2. The move from A to B in the graph above represents the substitution effect. As the wage rate goes up, the cost of leisure goes up due to an increase in its opportunity cost. Thus, the substitution effect of a wage increase will always be toward less leisure. If leisure is a normal good, the income effect of a wage increase would be toward the consumption of more leisure. Thus, if leisure is a normal good, the income and substitution effects of a wage increase go in opposite directions. Which effect is bigger will determine if work effort goes up or down in the face of a wage change.

Practice Problems for Chapter 7

1. Suppose you have an individual that consumes pizza almost every day. For this person, pizza is a Giffen good. Draw a graph showing the income and substitution effects with pizza on one axis and steak on the other axis for an increase in the price of pizza.

2. Draw an example of a simple Engel curve as income goes up for the consumption of pizza, if pizza is an inferior good. *not on test*

3. Assuming as in the text that a person can only work up to 16 hours per day. Draw a figure illustrating the income and substitution effects for a drop in the wage from $20 per hour to $10 per hour when leisure is an inferior good.

4. Draw a simple graph of the labor/leisure tradeoff for an individual who qualifies for a new tax rebate that will add $5000 to their income each year, regardless of how many hours are worked. Suppose leisure is a normal good, draw the income and substitution effects, if applicable. Would the person work harder after the imposition of the tax rebate? Suppose leisure is inferior, would your answer change?

Chapter 8

Production Costs, Revenues and Profit

In this chapter, we explore the cost structure for the firm and start to look at how the firm optimizes its production output given those costs. The firm's costs are segmented into several components. Table 8.1 below outlines the basic costs for a firm with the *cost function*—as its name sounds, a function describing how cost varies with output—equal to:

Eq. 8.1 $C = 50 + 3q^2$

Table 8.1
The Costs of Production for a Firm

Output	Fixed Cost	Variable Cost	Total Cost	Marginal Cost	Average Fixed Cost	Average Variable Cost	Average Total Cost
q	FC	VC	C	MC	AFC	AVC	AC
0	50	0	50	----	----	----	----
1	50	3	53	3	50	3	53
2	50	12	62	9	25	6	31
3	50	27	77	15	16.7	9	25.7
4	50	48	98	21	12.5	12	24.5
5	50	75	125	27	10	15	25
6	50	108	158	33	8.3	18	26.3
7	50	147	197	39	7.1	21	28.1

Fixed cost (FC) is the component of cost that doesn't vary with the level of output. In the cost function above, it is the constant (= 50). Sometimes economists refer to fixed costs as "sunk costs." These are costs that the owners of the firm can't get back under any circumstances. The other component of costs is called ***variable cost*** (VC). This part of cost varies with the level of output. Fixed cost plus variable cost equals ***total cost*** (C). Marginal cost is the increment to total cost for each additional unit of output (the change in cost for a change in q or $\Delta C/\Delta q$).

Figure 8.1
Short-Run Costs for a Typical Firm

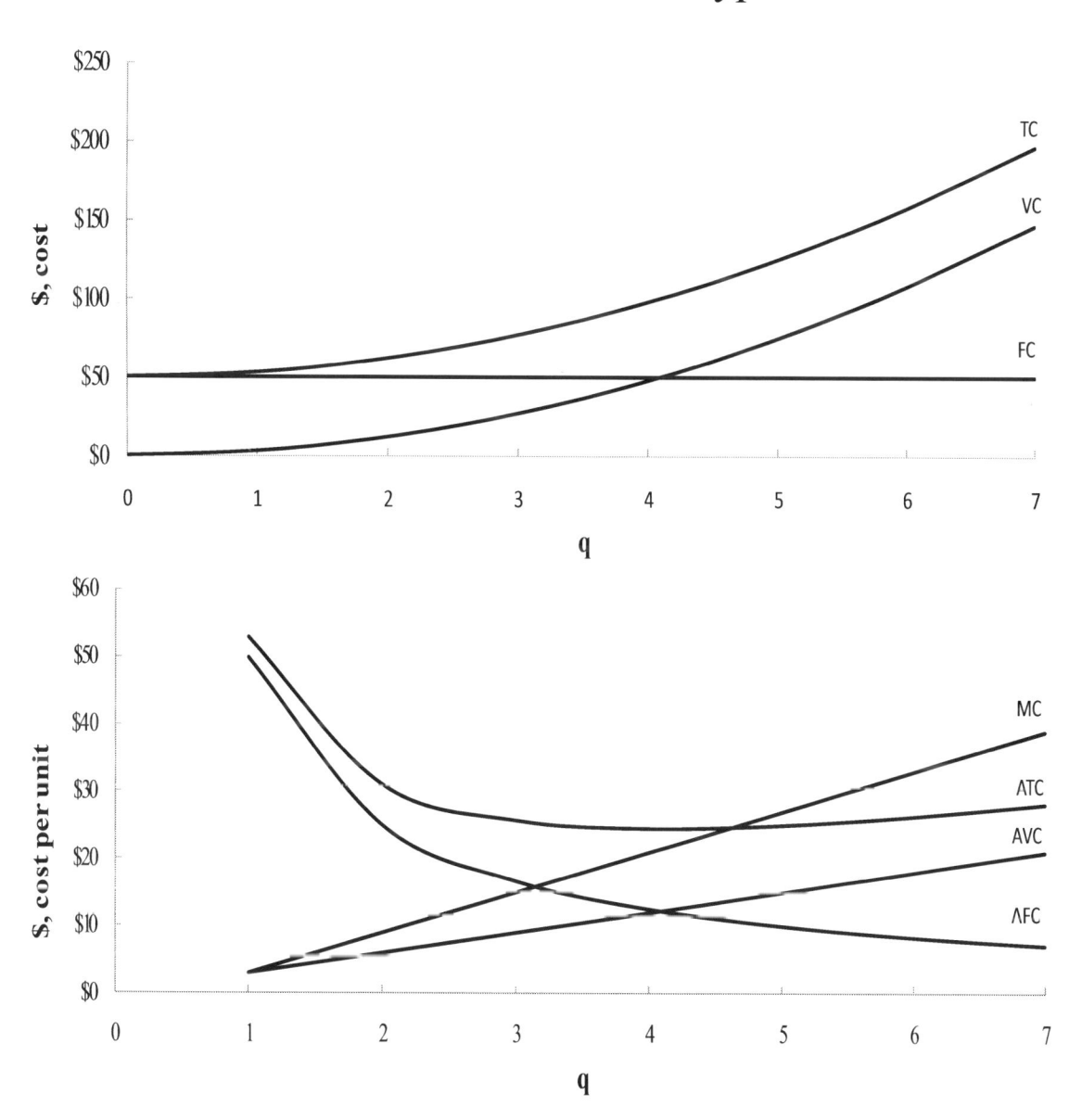

The next column in the table above is average fixed cost, which is calculated by taking fixed cost divided by q. Average variable cost is computed by dividing variable cost by q. Finally, average total cost can be computed either by adding average fixed cost plus average variable cost, or by dividing total cost by q.

The Effects of Taxes on the Firm's Cost Curves

In this section, we look at how taxation might affect a firm's cost curves. We start by looking at a per-unit tax on the firm's output. (See Figure 8.2 below.) Suppose a firm's output becomes subject to a tax of τ dollars per unit, whereas initially there was no tax. What would this do to the average and marginal cost curves? Can we tell if the point where the marginal cost curve bisects the average cost curve shifts left or right?

**Figure 8.2
A Per-Unit Tax on Output**

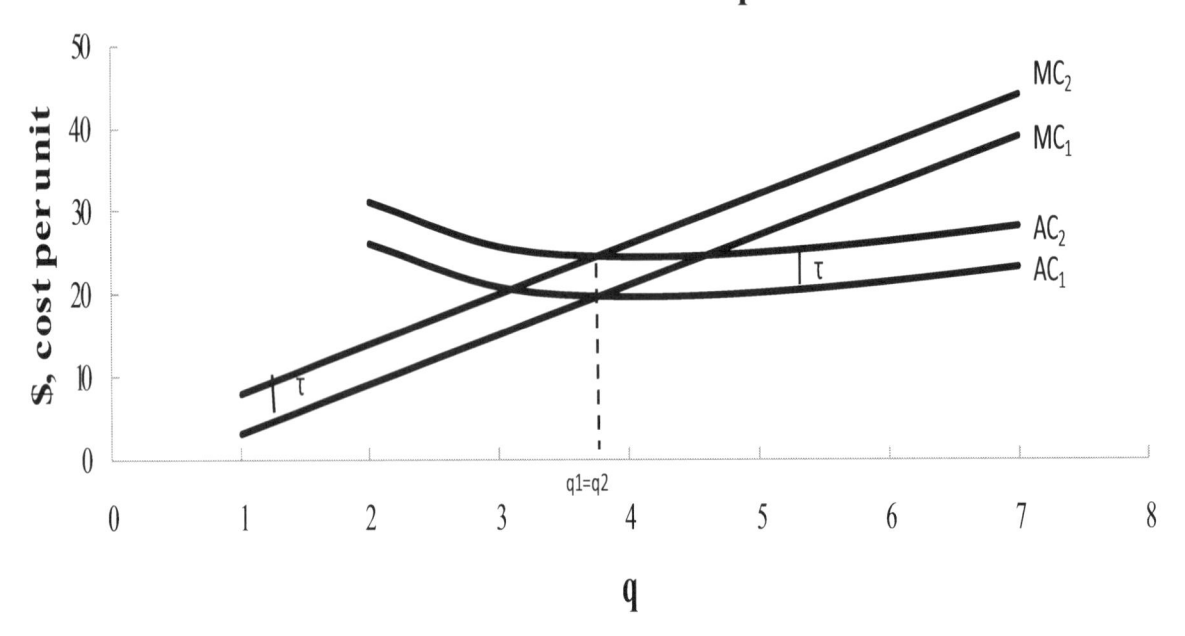

First, the average cost curve must be shifting vertically upward by the amount of the per-unit tax. Since the tax is added to each unit, the average cost must go up by τ. By the same reasoning, the marginal cost curve is shifted up vertically by the same amount. Since at the point of the initial intersection between AC_1 and MC_1, the average cost and marginal cost curves are shifted up vertically by τ, it must be true that the intersection of the two new curves is vertically above the old intersection by the amount τ as well.

Next, let's look at a slightly different kind of tax: a ***lump sum*** tax. This is a once and for all tax of a fixed amount. One example of a lump sum tax is sometimes referred to as a franchise tax. Let's suppose you are opening a fast food restaurant; you might have to pay a one-time fee to be able to use a certain brand for that restaurant. Another example might be if you are opening a securities broker business, you might be required to buy a license for that brokerage at the inception of business. Any type of a one-time tax of a fixed amount can be thought of as a lump sum tax. In Figure 8.3 below, we draw a graph of a firm's marginal and average cost curves with the imposition of a lump sum tax. Now, the marginal cost curve does not change because there is no additional cost per unit. The average cost curve is shifted up by the amount LS/q where LS represents the lump sum tax. The point of intersection between the two curves must shift to the right because the marginal cost curve is upward sloping and the average cost curve has shifted up.

**Figure 8.3
A Lump Sum Tax on a Firm**

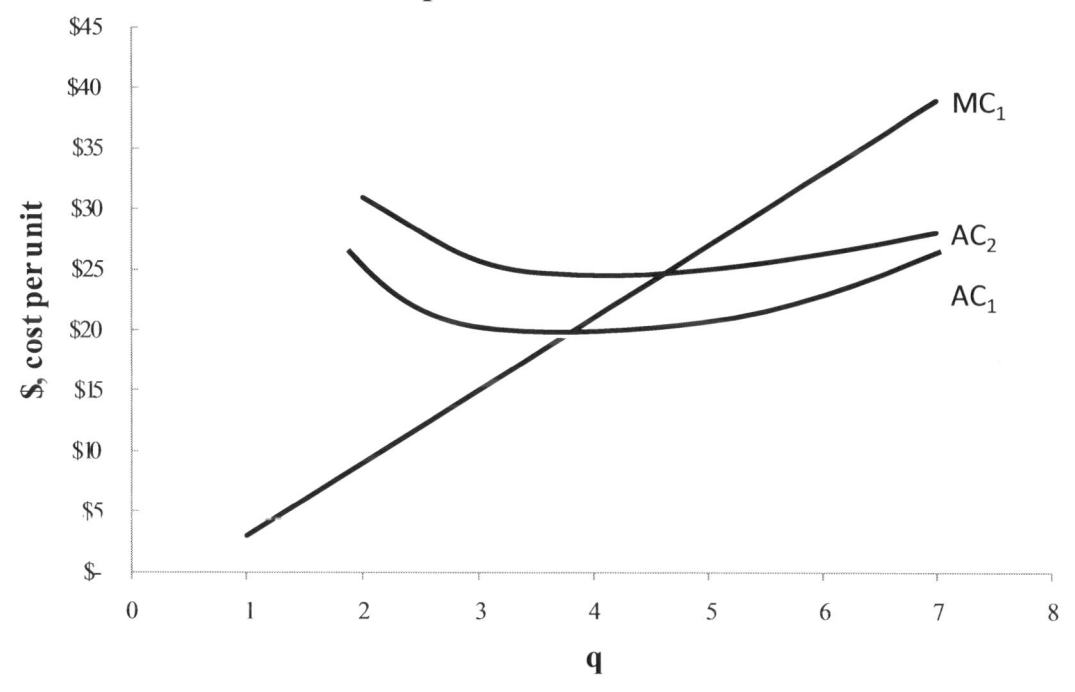

The Long-Run Average Cost Curve

We will see in the next chapter that the long-run competitive equilibrium for a firm is at the bottom of the long-run average cost curve.

For now, let's explore the relationship between the short-run average cost curves for a firm and the long-run average cost curve.

In many industries, firms may have a choice of technologies to employ in production. Firms are always searching for a competitive edge, so they tend to want to employ the most cost effective technologies. It makes sense that firms will tend to choose the method of production that will lead to the greatest ***profit*** (see section on revenues and profits below), and since profit is equal to ***revenue*** minus costs (where revenue is defined as price times quantity (or P x q), the lower the costs the greater the profit, ***ceteris paribus*** (all else equal).

In Figure 8.4, we see that the long-run average cost curve for a firm is really an envelope of all the possible short-run average cost curves. The lowest possible average cost will be at the bottom of this long-run average cost curve where dC/dq is equal to zero. Through competition, as we will see in the next chapter, firms will be driven to produce at the bottom of this envelope known as the long-run average cost curve.

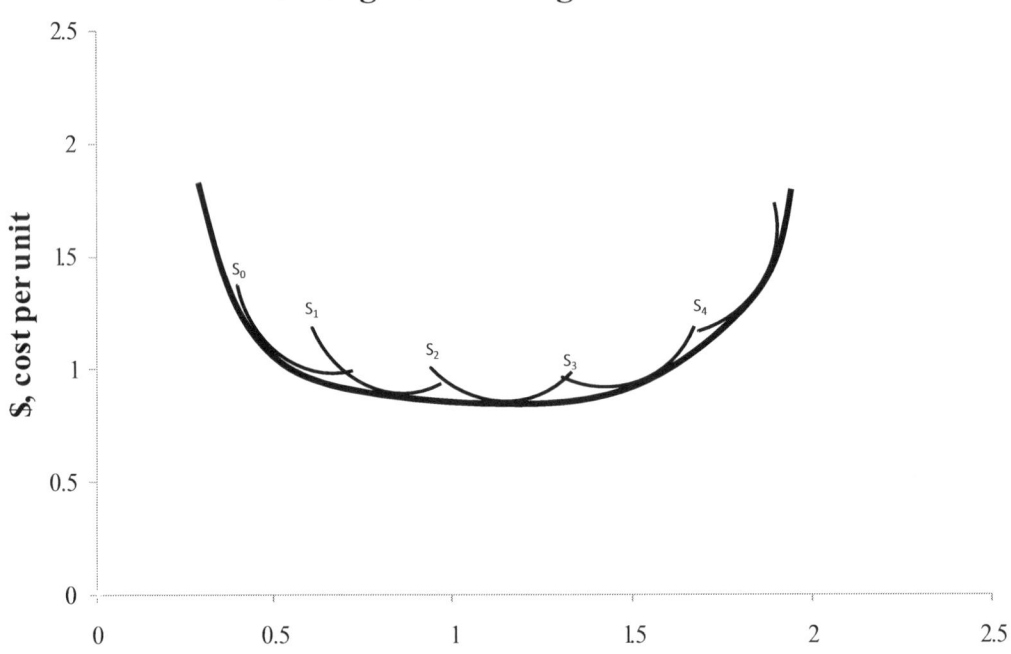

**Figure 8.4
The Long-Run Average Cost Curve**

Calculating Revenues and Profits

As stated above, the firm's revenues (**R**) are defined as price times quantity of output (P x q). It will be useful at times to calculate *marginal revenue*, which is the change in revenue for a change in the quantity of output or $\Delta R/\Delta q$.

Profits, which will be denoted by the Greek letter "π", are simply revenues minus costs (R – C).

Eq. 8.2 $\pi = R - C = (P \times q) - C$

If we multiply C from above by (q/q), we can rewrite Eq. 8.2 as:

Eq. 8.3 $\pi = (P \times q) - (C/q) \times q = (P \times q) - (AC \times q) = (P - AC) \times q$

This last expression for profits, (P – AC) x q, will be very useful to us when we try to calculate profits and/or graph profits in upcoming chapters, so try to remember it!!!

Practice Problems for Chapter 8

1. Suppose a firm has a cost function: $C = 5 + 2q^2 + q^3$.
   Draw a table like Table 8.1 for q between 0 and 4. Draw graphs similar to Figure 8.1, with one graph for FC, VC and C and another for MC, AFC, AVC, and AC.

2. If price is equal to $25 per unit, calculate R and π at each level of output for the problem above. At what level of output is profit maximized?

Chapter 9

Perfect Competition

In this chapter, we look at how the competitive firm optimizes its level of output in the short-run and long-run, and also examine the market equilibrium for firms in competitive industries. We start with the presumption that firms desire to maximize their profits (revenues minus costs) or at least minimize their losses. We will see that under some conditions, firms will continue to operate even if they are producing losses, but at other times it will be preferable to shut down.

For an industry to be deemed a competitive industry, it will have to demonstrate several characteristics including:

1) Free entry and exit
2) Many firms; individual firms do not have any impact on the price-- firms act as price takers
3) Firms are homogeneous; they produce the same product and utilize the same production technology
4) In the long-run, firms earn zero profits

Free entry and exit means that there are no significant barriers to entry in an industry and that when profits are above average, it can be expected that more firms will enter the market. Similarly, if profits are below normal, eventually firms will leave the market. There are many firms and thus no one firm can exert any influence on the price by itself.

When we say that firms earn zero profits in the long-run, it really means that firms tend to earn the "normal" rate of return in the long-run. To make things easier for modeling purposes, economists normalize long-run profits as being zero.

In Figure 9.1 below, we see that the competitive firm will maximize profits (or minimize losses) by setting choosing to produce the quantity of output (q*) where marginal cost equals marginal revenue. This has to be the optimum for the firm because if marginal cost is below marginal revenue, it will always make sense to produce more output. On the other hand, no firm will want to produce a unit of output if marginal cost is greater than marginal revenue.

Figure 9.1
Short-Run Profit Maximization for a Competitive Firm

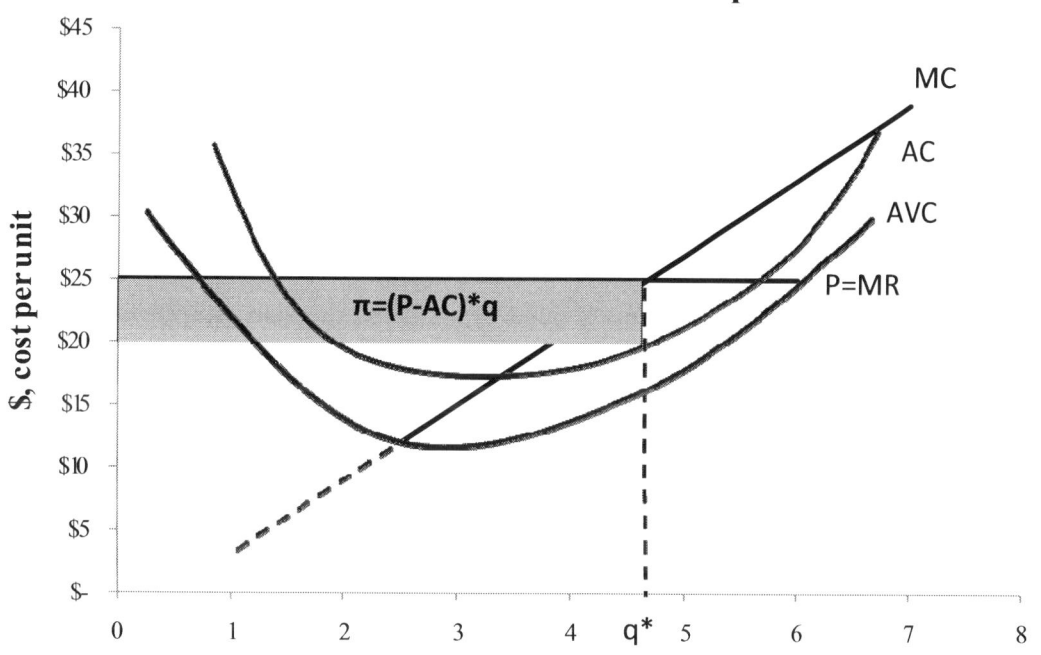

Figure 9.1
Short-Run Profit Maximization for a Competitive Firm

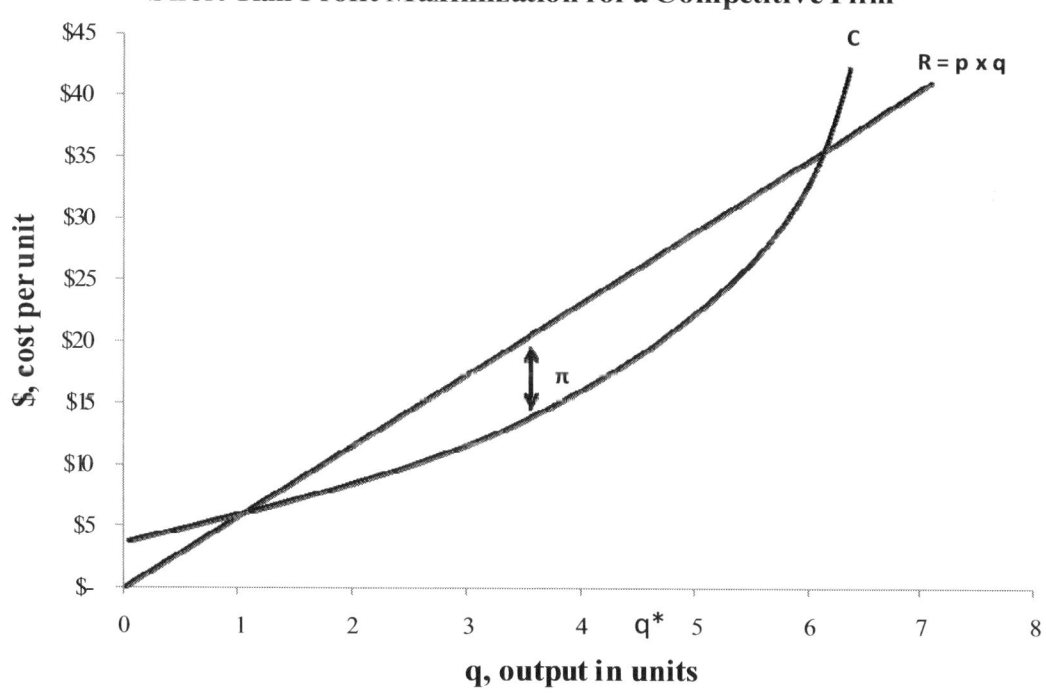

For the competitive firm, the price is given in the marketplace and no individual firm can influence the price. Thus, since price is given, it has to be true that marginal revenue is equal to the price. Each unit of output earns the marginal revenue, P.

In Figure 9.2 below, we can see how the marginal cost curve becomes the supply curve for the firm. As the price rises, which is equal to marginal revenue for the competitive firm also, the firm will set marginal cost equal to marginal revenue. Thus, the marginal cost curve becomes the supply curve for the competitive firm.

Figure 9.2
Short-Run Supply Curve for the Competitive Firm

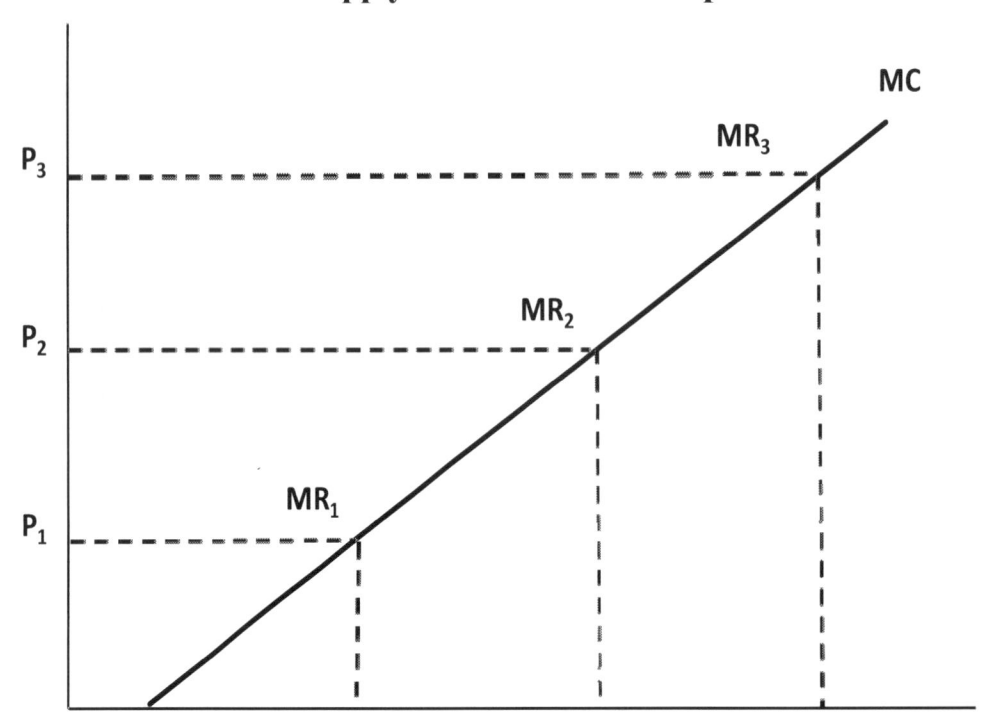

The Short-Run and Long-Run Shutdown Rules for a Firm

The short-run decision for a firm to either keep producing or shut down is quite easy:

Short-Run Shutdown Rule: if P < AVC, shut down.

Since fixed costs are sunk costs, they don't enter into the shutdown decision.

In Figure 9.3 below, the firm optimizes its output decision by setting MC = MR. As long as P is greater than AVC, the firm will continue to produce output. In Figure 9.3, the firm will continue to operate even though it is operating at a loss. The shaded area in the graph represents fixed costs. If the firm shuts down, its loss will be equal to fixed costs or areas A plus B in the figure. When the firm continues to operate, its loss becomes equal to the part of the shaded area above P (area A). Although it is still operating at a loss, the loss is smaller than if it stops production entirely.

In the long run, all costs become like variable costs. Therefore, there are no fixed costs. The shutdown rule in the long run is again quite simple:

Long-Run Shutdown Rule: if P < AC, shut down.

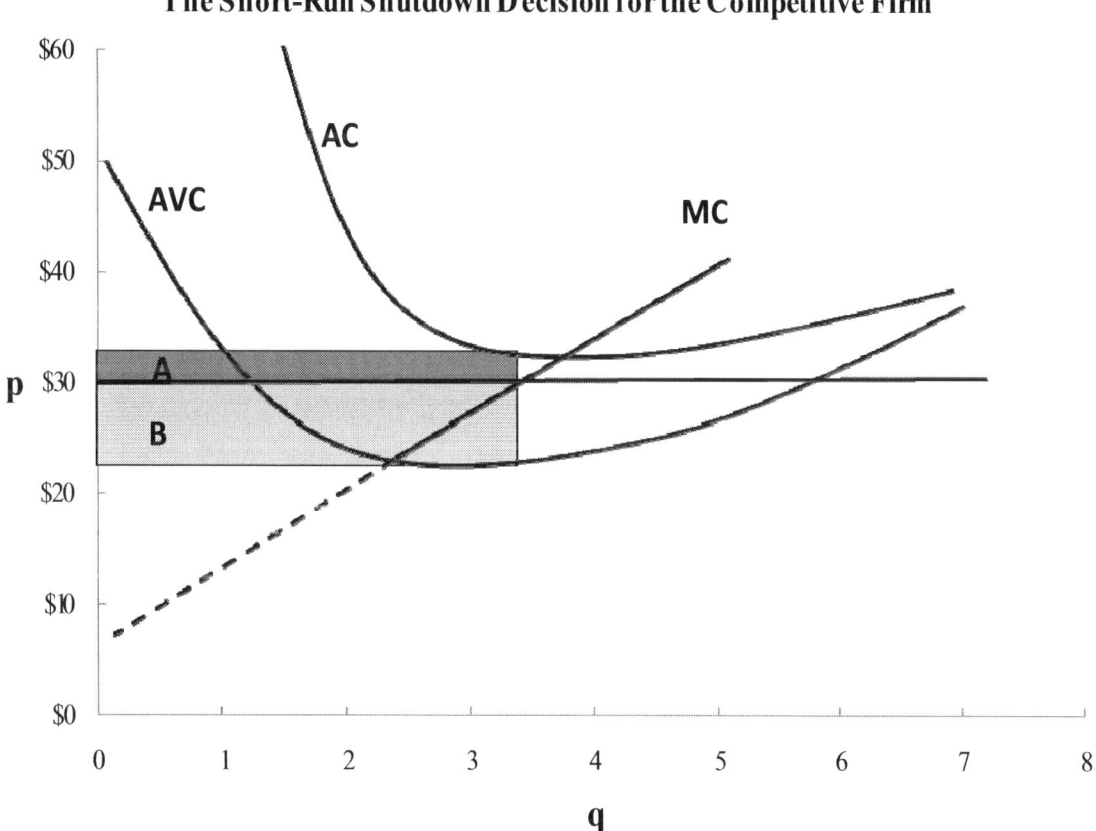

Figure 9.3
The Short-Run Shutdown Decision for the Competitive Firm

The Supply Curve for a Competitive Industry

In this section of the text, we examine the relationship between the supply curve for the individual firm and the supply curve for the industry. We will assume that the firms are identical (homogeneous) in a competitive industry. In Figure 9.4 below, we see the supply curve for the firm and for the industry where there are five identical firms. In practice, we expect most competitive industries to have many more firms than that, but for purposes of simplification, we are assuming that there are five firms here.

Figure 9.4
The Short-Run Supply Curve for the Firm

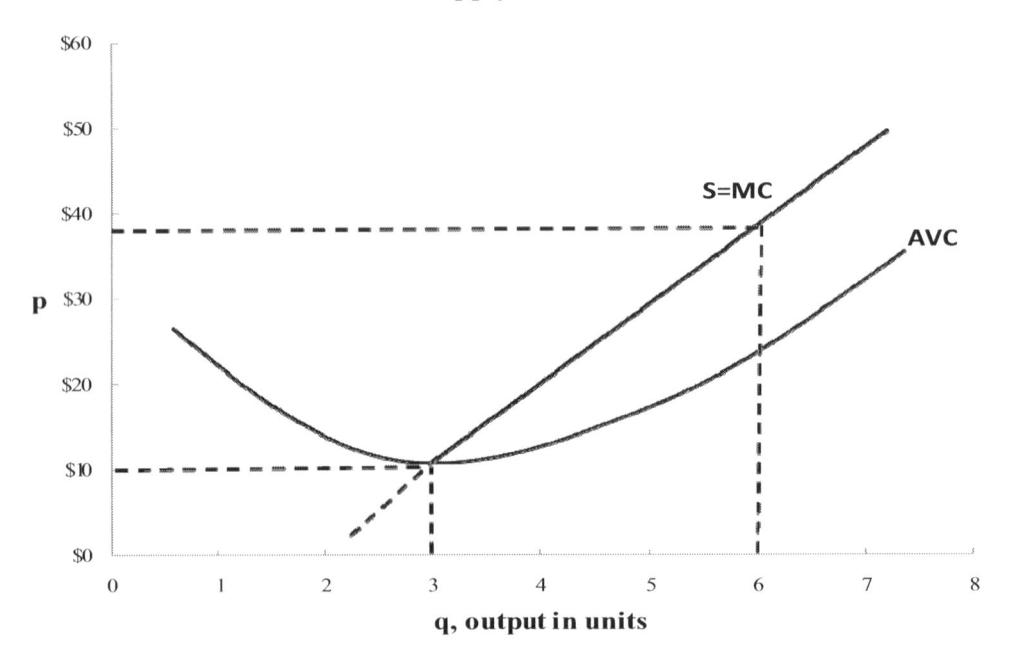

Figure 9.4
The Short-Run Supply Curve for the Industry
(Five Identical Firms)

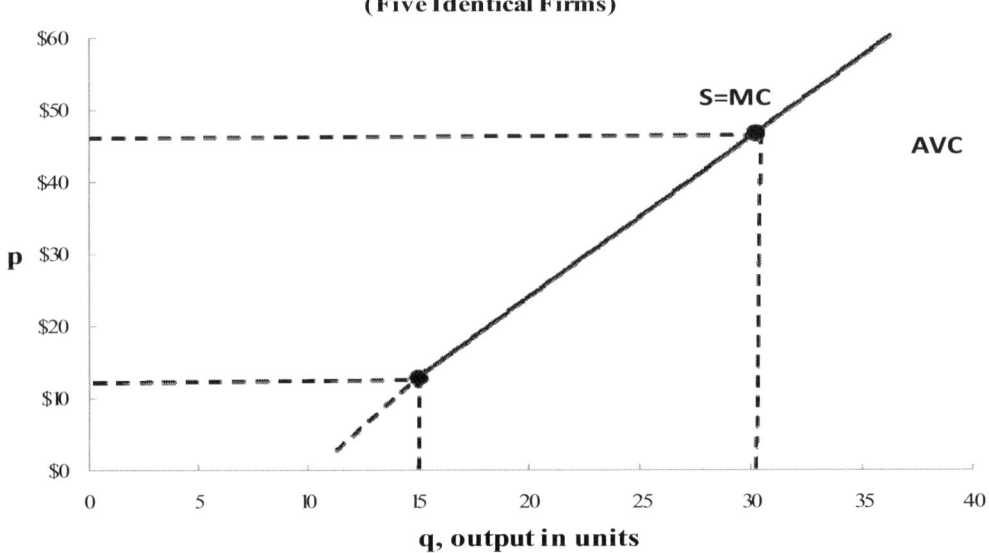

The supply curve for the industry is derived by multiplying the output level of the individual firm by 5 at each price (since there are 5 firms). In this manner, we are able to derive the supply curve for the industry.

In Figure 9.5, we examine the impact of an increase in the cost of an input (wheat) on the firm and industry supply curves in long-run equilibrium. The increase in the price of wheat causes both the average cost and the marginal cost curves to shift up. Since they both shift up by the same amount, the new equilibrium shifts vertically up as well.

Figure 9.5
An Increase in the Cost of Wheat in the Bread Baking Industry
(Long-Run Equilibrium)

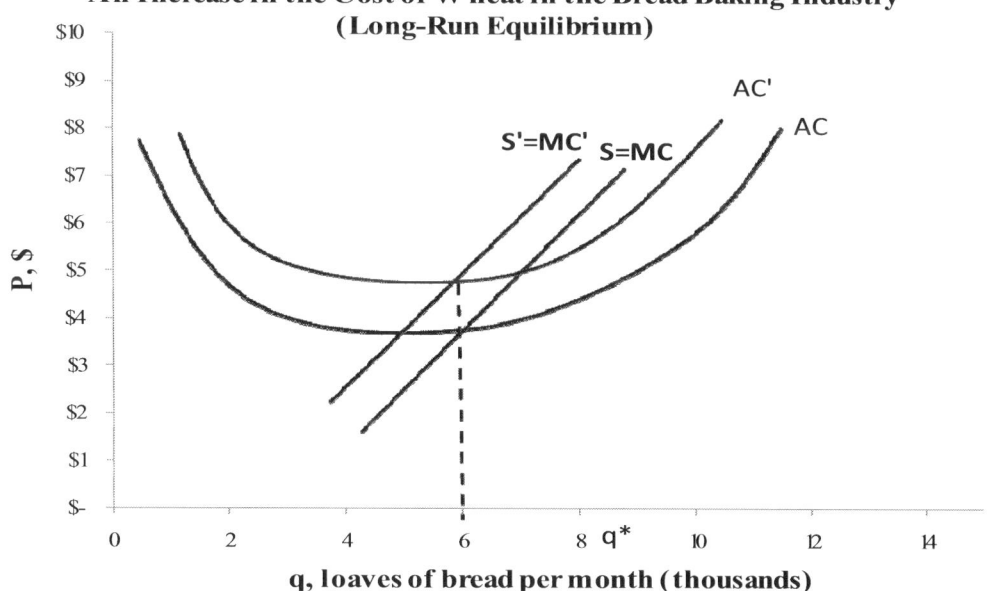

Figure 9.5
An Increase in the Cost of Wheat in the Bread Baking Industry
(Long-Run Equilibrium)

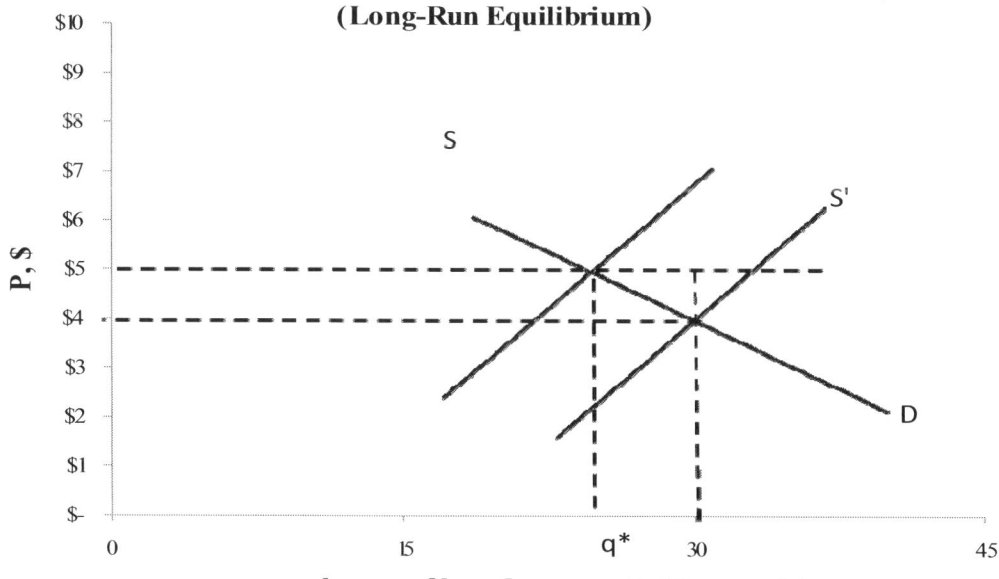

In Figure 9.6 below, we see that the long-run supply curve for an industry is determined by technology. Firms are constrained to have zero profits in the long-run. They must operate where P = AC at the base of the long-run average cost curve. If the price is above the minimum of the average cost curves, more firms will enter driving the price down. If the price is less than the minimum of the AC curve, firms will exit the market allowing the price to rise back up to the long-run equilibrium level at the minimum of the AC curve.

**Figure 9.6
Long-Run Market Supply Determined by Technology**

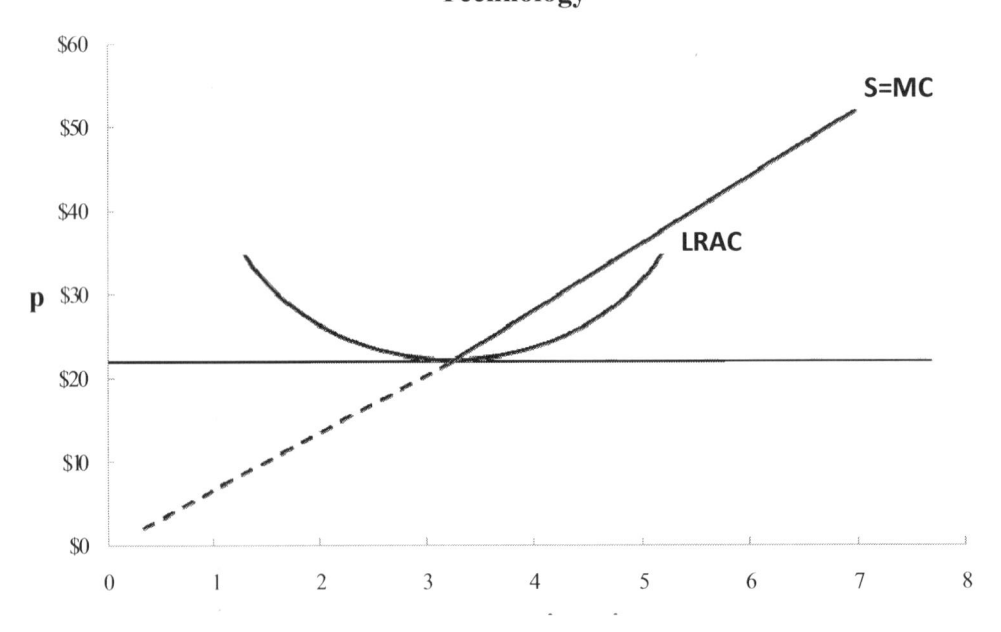

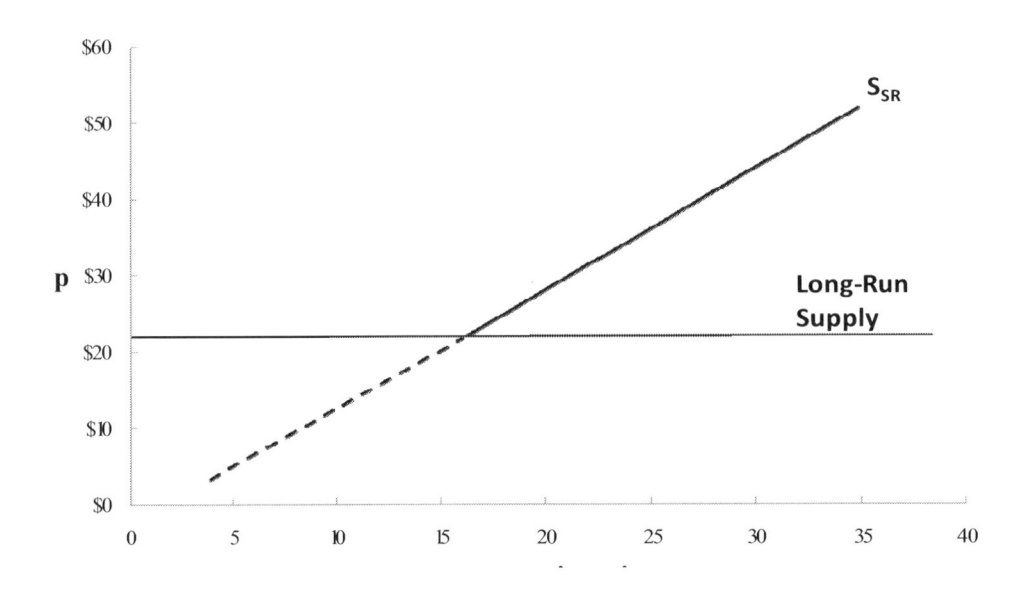

9.7

In Figure 9.7, we explore how the short-run determination of profits and losses is made. When demand is relatively strong and the price is P_2, the firm sets MC = MR and is able to produce a significant profit. Profit is represented in the figure by the shaded area (A) which mathematically would be given by $(P - AC) \times Q$.

When demand is weaker (demand curve D'), the price falls to P_1 and since $P_1 < AC$, the firm is now generating losses represented by the other shaded area (B) in the figure.

Figure 9.7
Profits and (Losses) in the Short-Run with a Shift in Demand

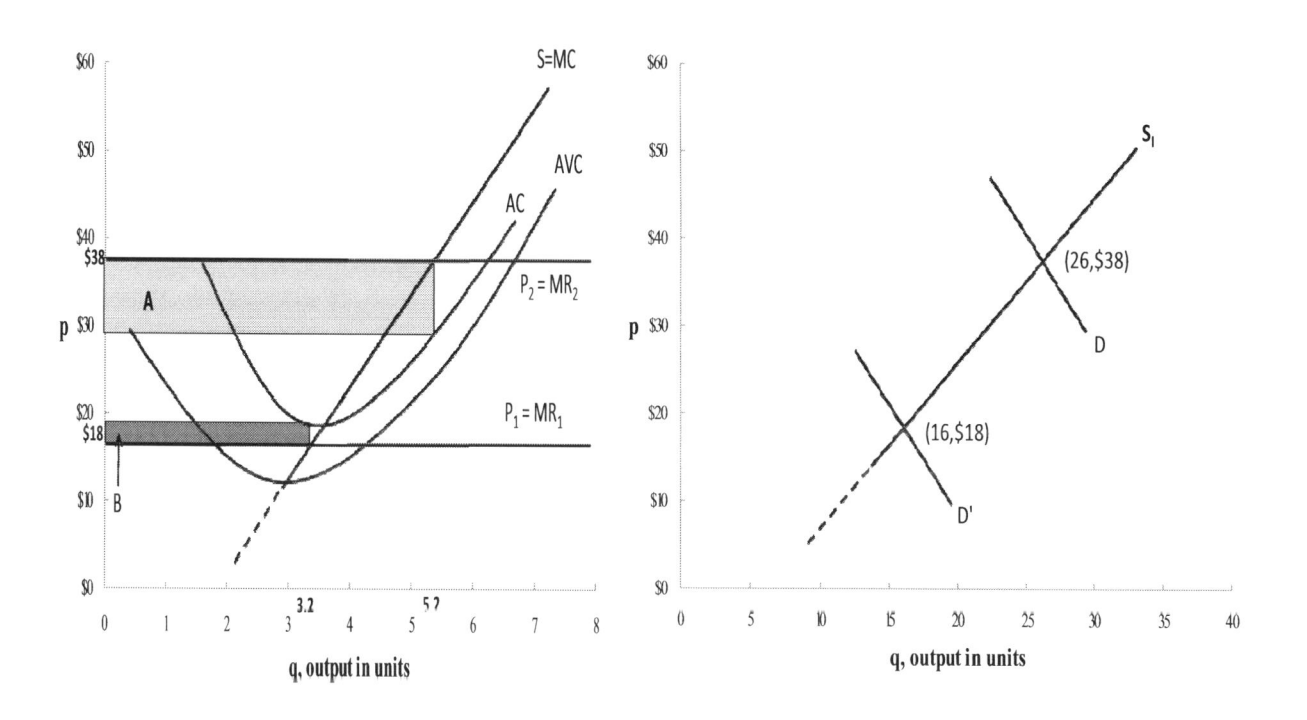

Practice Problems for Chapter 9

1. Draw a simple graph (or graphs) showing why the long-run supply curve in a competitive industry is horizontal. Explain

2. Why does the marginal cost curve represent the supply curve for a competitive firm, but only above average variable cost?

3. Why do competitive firms sometimes continue to operate even though they are operating at a loss? Draw a graph showing this situation and explain why the firm is better off continuing to produce output.

Chapter 10

Monopoly

For the competitive firm, the price is determined by the market and the individual firm has no impact on the price. With only one firm producing output in a given industry—the definition of monopoly--this assumption that the firm acts as a price taker can no longer hold. Also, since now there is only one firm in the market, when the firm increases its output, this will tend to drive the price downward. Thus, both the demand curve and the marginal revenue curve will be downward sloping for the monopoly firm.

In Figure 10.1, we see the relationship between demand and marginal revenue for the monopolist firm. We also illustrate the elasticity of demand along the demand curve for the monopolist.

Figure 10.1
The Demand and Marginal Revenue Curves
For a Monopolist

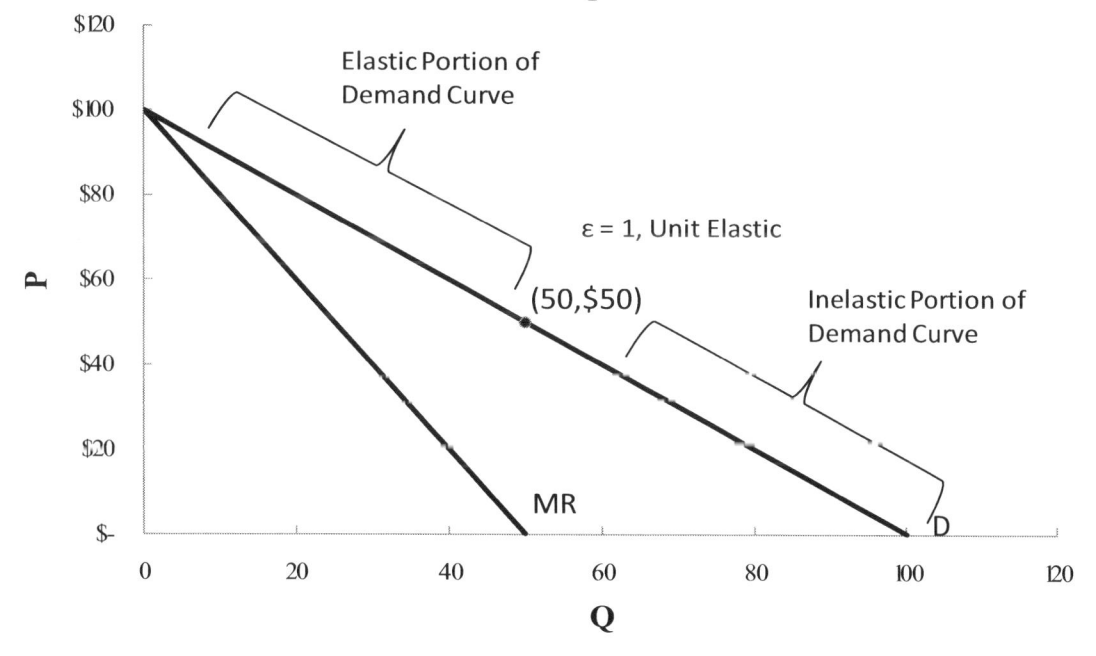

Solving for the Monopolist's Optimum

The monopolist will maximize profit by setting marginal revenue equal to marginal cost. This is the same profit maximizing condition as for the competitive firm, and we will later see for the oligopolist as well. As long as marginal revenue is above marginal cost, the monopolist can increase profit by increasing output. Thus, the monopolist will continue to increase output just until the point that MR = MC.

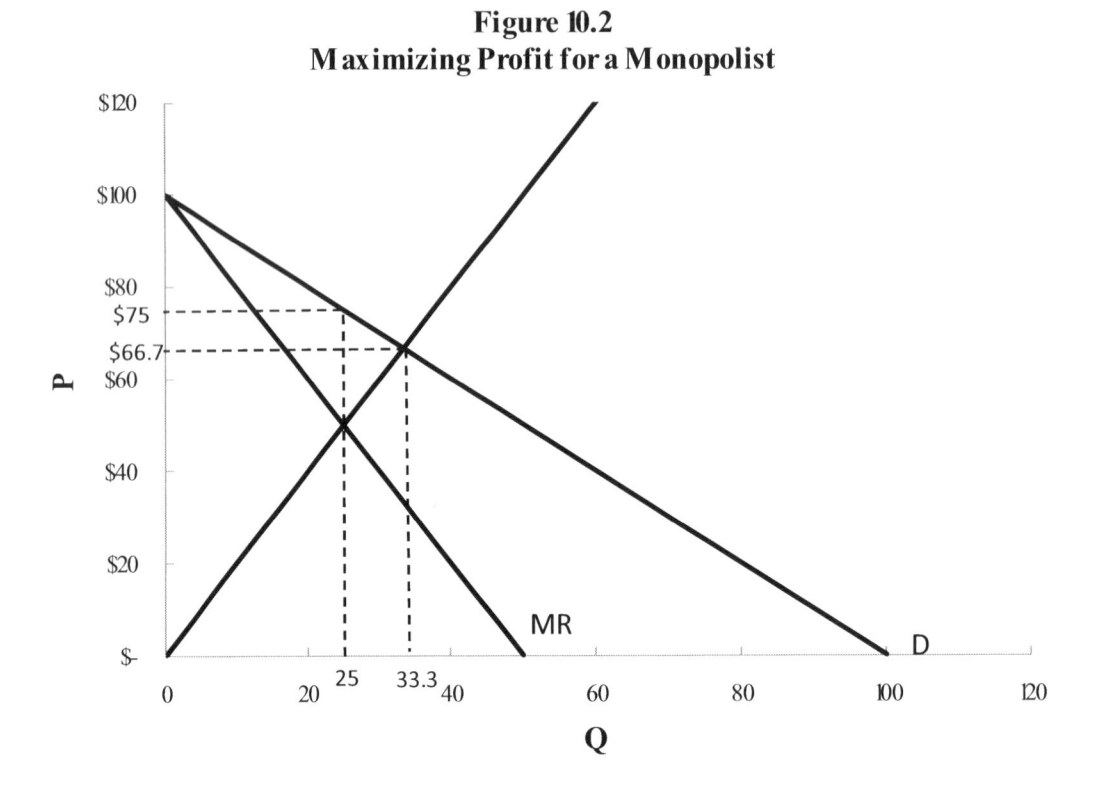

**Figure 10.2
Maximizing Profit for a Monopolist**

Measuring Monopoly Power

There are two measures of monopoly power that we will use in this text: 1) the price/marginal cost ratio, and 3) the "Lerner Index."

Table 10.1
Measures of Monopoly Power

	Price/Marginal Cost Ratio (P/MC)	Lerner Index $(P - MC)/P = -(1/\varepsilon)$
Greater Monopoly Power	11	0.91
	1.25	0.20
Less Monopoly Power	1.01	0.01
	1.00	0

As we can see above, the greater the price/marginal cost ratio the greater the monopoly power. When the P/MC ratio is equal to one, the industry is perfectly competitive. For the Lerner Index, the closer to one, the greater the monopoly power. The perfectly competitive industry will have a Lerner Index of 0.

Welfare Loss from Monopoly

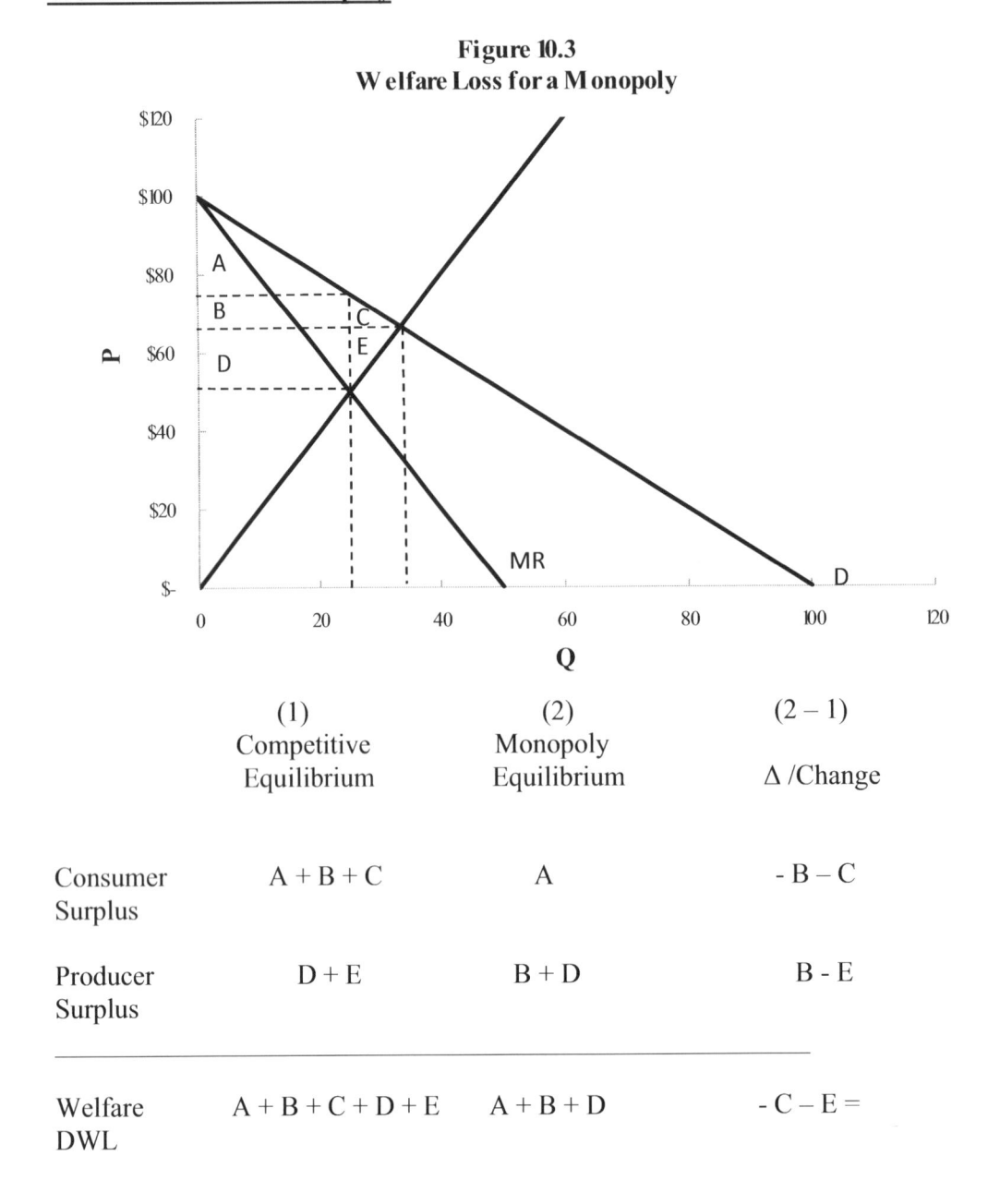

Figure 10.3
Welfare Loss for a Monopoly

	(1) Competitive Equilibrium	(2) Monopoly Equilibrium	(2 – 1) Δ /Change
Consumer Surplus	A + B + C	A	– B – C
Producer Surplus	D + E	B + D	B – E
Welfare DWL	A + B + C + D + E	A + B + D	– C – E =

In Figure 10.3 above, we show the welfare loss from a monopoly. The competitive equilibrium is where the demand and marginal cost/supply curves cross. In the monopoly situation, the monopolist is able to estimate their downward sloping marginal revenue curve and set output where MC = MR. This leads to a lower level of output, a higher price for the consumer and a deadweight loss (– C – E).

In Figure 10.4, we can see that a patent can lead to large profits for a monopolist. The marginal cost of producing a tablet or pharmaceutical may be small relative to the price the holder of the patent is able to get for that product.

Is it beneficial to society to allow drug makers to have an incentive to invest in research and development? In Figure 10.4, the pharmaceutical company sells the tablets for more than 10 times their marginal cost showing strong monopoly power and profits are large as well. This provides incentive for the firm to keep investing in R&D to churn out more life-saving drugs in the future.

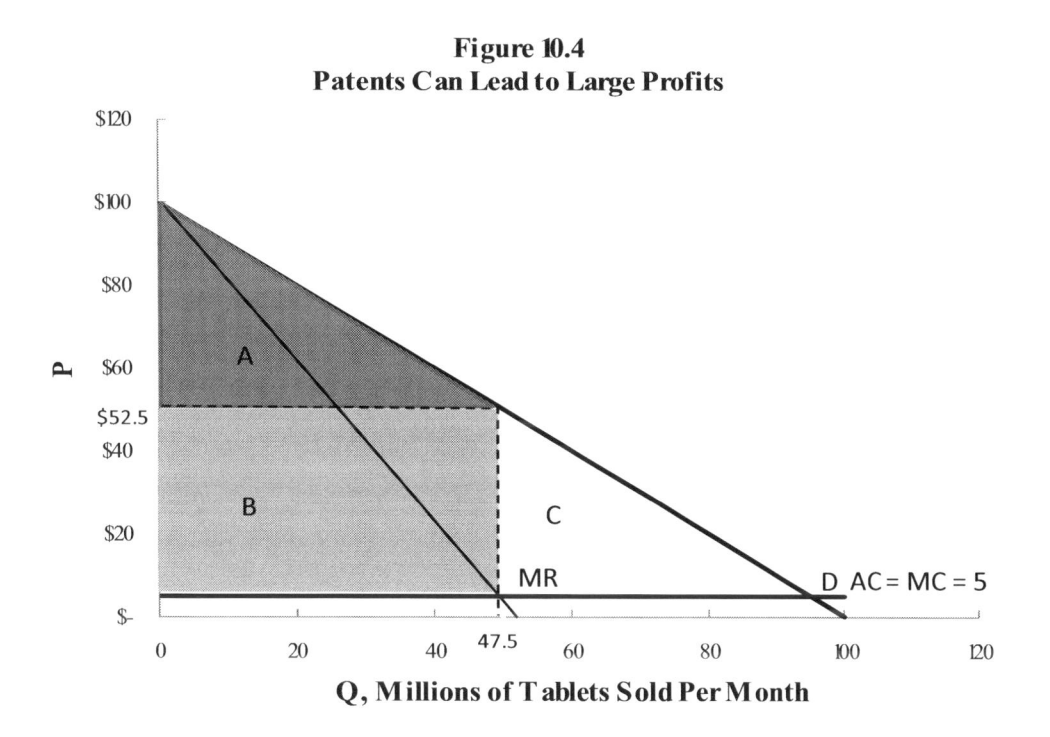

Figure 10.4
Patents Can Lead to Large Profits

Optimal Regulation of Monopolies

In many instances, it is better to regulate monopolies than to forbid them to operate and/or try to break them apart. For example, when there are economies of scale in a given industry, it is more socially beneficial to allow monopolies to continue to operate to allow them to develop the greatest scale and be able to lower the price to the consumer with regulation. When the average cost curve is always downward sloping for a firm, we say we have a ***natural monopoly***. In this case, regulation is the answer, not breaking the firm into many pieces.

In Figure 10.5 below, we see a firm with a natural monopoly structure. The average cost curve slopes downward at all points. Optimal regulation would either require setting the average cost equal to the price in which case profits would be zero, or setting marginal cost equal to the price, in which case it would be necessary to subsidize the firm to them back up to zero profits. (They would be incurring a loss where MC = P < AC; area B in the figure below.) On the other hand, without regulation the monopoly would reduce output, causing the price to rise and profits would also rise (area A).

Figure 10.5
Optimal Regulation of a Natural Monopoly

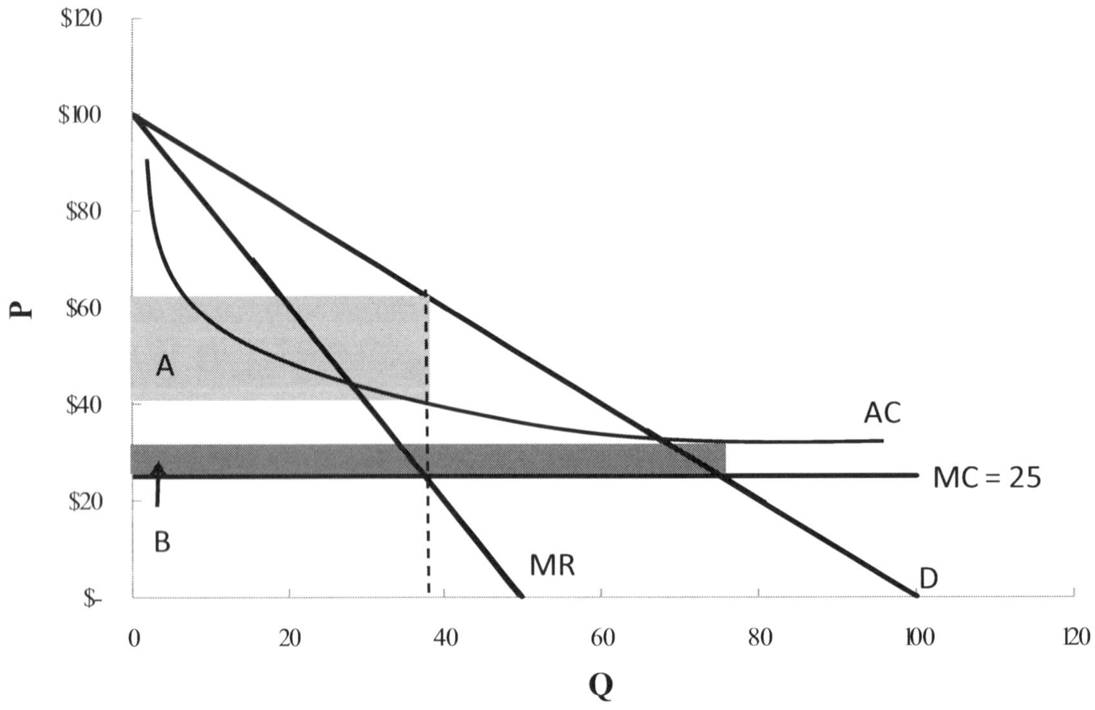

Price-Discriminating Monopolist

In some circumstances, a monopolist may be able to increase its profits by dividing the market for its product in segments and optimizing each segment of the market independently. In order for the monopolist to be able to do this some conditions must hold:

Conditions for Price-Discriminating Monopoly Power:

1) the firm must have some monopoly power (i.e., it can't produce a homogeneous product that other firms can produce cost effectively)
2) the firm must be able to gauge the different segments of its market and be able to have some insight into the elasticity of demand in those segments, and
3) the firm must be able to prevent resales.

In order for the firm to be able to price discriminate, it must be a monopolist—at least to some extent. The firm must have some knowledge of its customer base and the different segments of its market must have differing characteristics with regard to their price responsiveness. Finally, the firm must be able to stop other firms or individuals from buying products in one market in order to resell in another market. For example, if a restaurant wishes to provide "early bird" special prices to seniors, it must be able to distinguish between seniors and other individuals (through the use of I.D.s, etc.).

In Figure 10.7 below, we lay out the problem for a book publisher who sells books in the US and Indian markets. The price discriminating monopolist is able to increase profits relative to a "single price monopolist" by setting MC = MR in each market. (Note that, generally, marginal cost will be the same in each market but the marginal revenue curves will be different.)

Figure 10.7
Profit Maximization for a Price Discriminating Monopolist

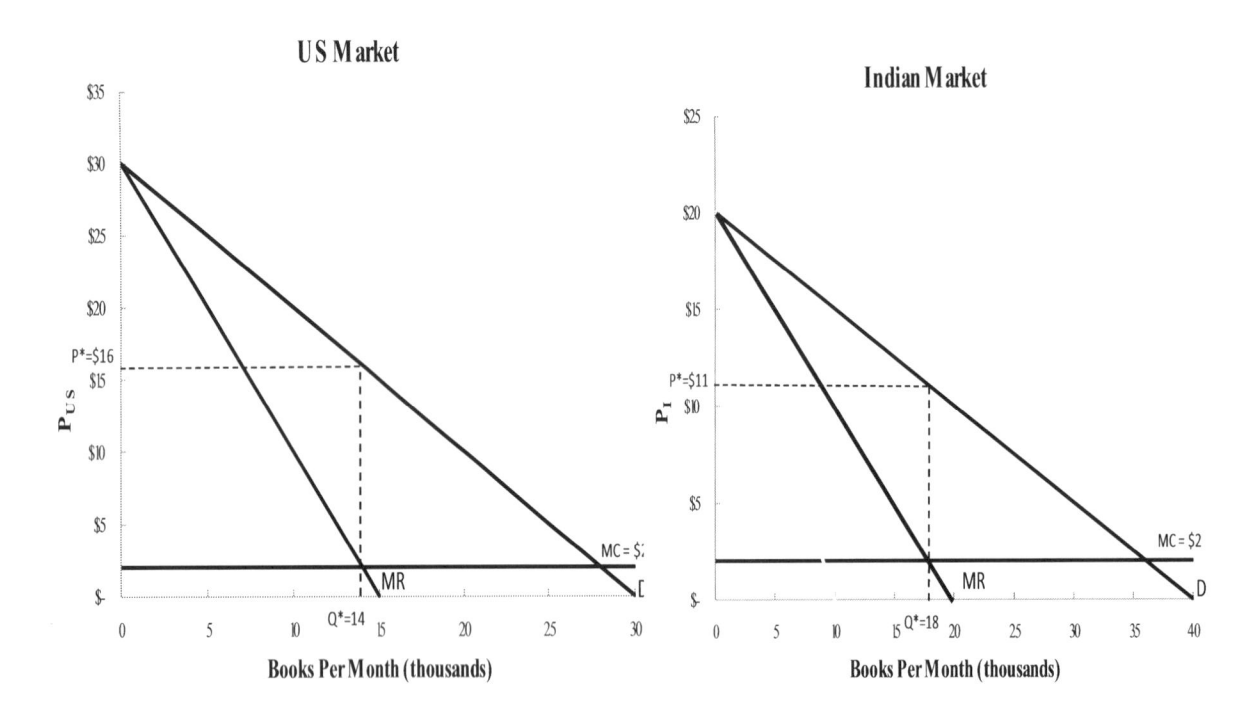

Practice Problems for Chapter 10

1. Suppose you find that a 1 liter of saline costs about 10 cents to make. A hospital charges $12.00 per liter of saline used for intravenous purposes. Calculate the price/marginal cost ratios and Lerner Index for a liter of saline. How do you think the hospital justifies the charges?

2. Will an unregulated monopolist operate in the elastic or inelastic portion of the demand curve? Why don't they operate where revenue is maximized and elasticity is unit elastic?

3. What is similar and what is different about the (long-run) monopoly and competitive equilibriums?

4. For what types of industries will the government generally allow monopolies to persist? Why do they do this and is there a need for regulation in these industries?

Chapter 11

Oligopoly and Strategic Behavior by Firms

In this chapter, we look at the oligopoly structure for firms. Will the equilibrium look closer to the monopoly equilibrium or the purely competitive equilibrium? In the industry structures of monopoly and perfect competition, there was one dominant strategy that won out and the equilibrium was very predictable. With oligopoly, the outcome is less certain and depends on the ability of firms to share information and/or cooperate.

Overview of Market Structures

Before delving into our discussion of oligopoly, it is helpful to compare and contrast the equilibrium conditions for the different market structures. Table 11.1 does this.

Table 11.1

	Monopoly	Oligopoly	Monopolistic Competition	Perfect Competition
Market Power	Much	Some	Little	None
Relationship between Price and Marginal Cost	P > MC	P > MC	P > MC	P = MC
Profit Max. Condition	MC = MR	MC = MR	MC = MR	MC = MR
Slope of Marginal Revenue Curve	Downward Sloping	Downward Sloping	Downward Sloping	Horizontal
Ability to Set Price	Price Setter	Price Setter	Price Setter	Price Taker
Entry Conditions	No entry	Limited Entry	Free Entry	Free Entry
Long-run Profit	> 0	> 0	= 0	= 0
Product Differentiation	Single Product	Single Product	Differentiated Product	Homogeneous Product

Cartels

It will become clear that the best possible outcome for an oligopoly is to act like a monopoly. If firms are able to collude, they will restrict output relative to the competitive equilibrium. This will lead to a higher price and higher profits.

In the United States, and other countries, there are laws to prohibit collusion on price. Firms are required to price their output and set their level of output on their own. Sometimes *cartels* will form to act more like monopolists. Cartels are groups of firms that collude in setting prices and/or output levels. Some cartels, such as OPEC (the Organization of Petroleum Exporting Countries), operate without prosecution. Even though the United States has incentives to prohibit cartels from operating, it realizes that it would be impossible to keep OPEC from operating as a cartel. Suppose the United States refused to buy oil from OPEC. OPEC would just sell it to somebody else who would then resell it to the US.

There is the most incentive to form cartels when there are a relatively few firms in an industry, when the output of the industry is homogeneous, and, obviously, when there is a lack of enforcement or laws against cartels.

Strategic Behavior by Firms/Simple Game Theory

When there are laws against collusion, firms will try to maximize their level of profit but their profits will be dependent to a large extent on the behavior of other firms. Pricing behavior in the real world is extremely complex. We will try to simplify our examination of pricing behavior by firms under oligopoly conditions using *game theory*. Game theory is a branch of mathematical economics which attempts to model how individuals and/or firms behave under different circumstances. A *game* is a one or more period economic event in which *players* are trying to optimize their outcomes, but generally with some kind of restriction on the amount of information that is available to them. A *Nash equilibrium* is an equilibrium from a one or more period game, where each player attempts to optimize the outcome for his/herself, holding other players' behavior constant. A *Cournot equilibrium* is a type of Nash equilibrium, where the other players' quantities of output are held constant.

Just as with almost every other economic model, we make some simplifying assumptions to start. Let us start with a Cournot *duopoly* (where there are only two firms in an industry). Suppose we have an automobile industry with only two firms: Board Motors and Federal Motors. Suppose also that their profit (in millions of dollars) is given in the following matrix (Figure 11.1). Federal Motors can choose either high or low output, but will optimize holding the output level of Board Motors constant and Board Motors will optimize holding the output level of Federal Motors constant.

If Board Motors chooses first and they choose high output, Federal Motors would have a choice between high output (profit = $3.1 million) or low output (profit = $2.9 million). Of course, since $3.1 million is greater than $2.9 million, they would choose high output. If Board Motors had chosen low output, Federal Motors would still have chosen high output since $5.0 million is greater than $4.4 million. Thus, we say the ***dominant strategy***, the strategy that Federal Motors will take regardless of what Board Motors does, is to choose high output. It turns out that the dominant strategy for Board Motors is also high output. (Try to go through the reasoning yourself, looking first at Federal Motors choosing high output and then low output. How would Board Motors respond?)

Notice that the upper left quadrant that is reached in this Cournot duopoly equilibrium is not the best possible outcome for the two companies. If the two companies had each chosen low output, each of their profits would have been higher. What prevents the two companies from reaching the preferable outcome? They are not able to share information and respond only to the other firms behavior and hold that behavior constant when selecting their optimal level of output.

We can see from this simple example that firms in an oligopoly market structure may not reach the best possible equilibrium with regard to maximizing profits. If firms are prohibited from colluding on price and output levels, strategic behavior will be very important in determining the equilibrium and in many cases the outcomes may be suboptimal from the firm's perspectives. To some extent, this explains the price wars in the airline industry and/or other industries. Sometimes pricing behavior can seem irrational, but firms are involved in a complex, repeated game and they are unable to collude to reach a better outcome.

Figure 11.1
Cournot Duopoly Dilemma

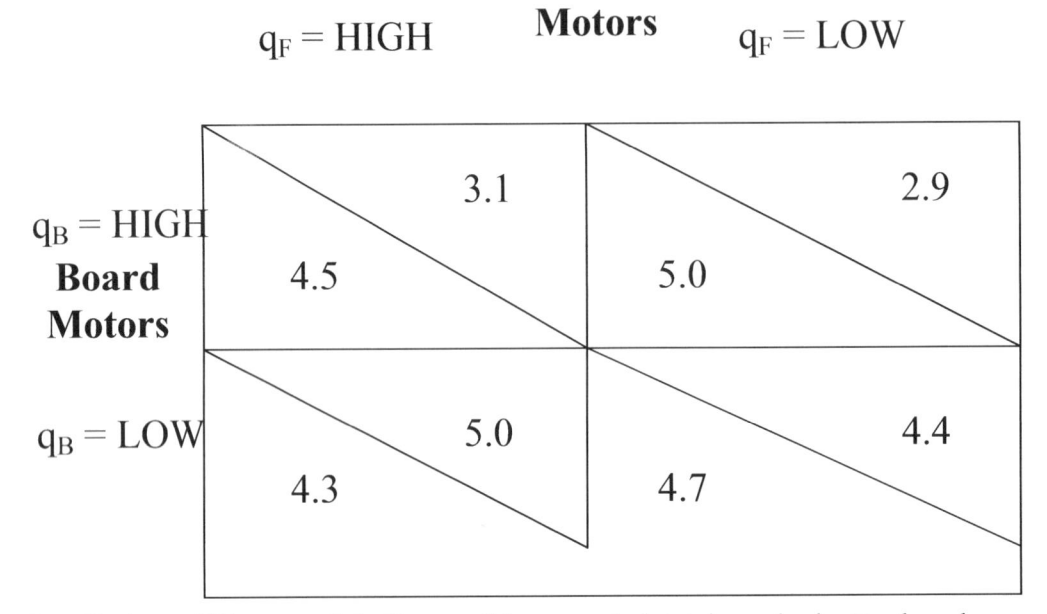

	Federal Motors	
	q_F = HIGH	q_F = LOW
Board Motors q_B = HIGH	4.5 / 3.1	5.0 / 2.9
q_B = LOW	4.3 / 5.0	4.7 / 4.4

Notes: Profit in millions of dollars. Upper-right triangle is Federal Motors profit. Lower-left triangle is Board Motors profit.

Practice Problems for Chapter 11

1. Sometimes the Cournot game outlined in Table 13.2 is referred to as the prisoner's dilemma. Suppose you have two mob suspects, Moe and Larry, that are picked up by the police and escorted to separate cells for questioning. Moe's lawyer advises him of the likely outcomes for his prospective sentencing in terms of years of jail time as follows:

    Moe's Sentencing Prospects

confess	Moe confesses	Moe doesn't
If Larry confesses:	9 yrs.	11 yrs.
If Larry doesn't confess	3 yrs.	5 yrs.

    Likewise, Larry's attorney advises him of his sentencing prospects:

    Larry's Sentencing Prospects

confess	Larry confesses	Larry doesn't
If Moe confesses:	11 yrs.	12 yrs.
If Moe doesn't confess	6 yrs.	7 yrs.

    Draw the diagram similar to Table 13.2 and discuss whether they reach the optimal outcome. Why or why not? What relevance does this have to firm pricing and why we don't allow firms to collude when setting their prices?

2. Discuss why OPEC (Oil and Petroleum Exporting Countries) might function less effectively as a cartel when the world economy is in recession.

Chapter 12
Monopolistic Competition

In the "real world," probably very few industries look exactly like the perfectly competitive model, we have looked at. In reality, firms try to differentiate their product to attract customers and develop brand loyalty in many instances. Firms try to legally attain monopoly power through new product development. However, when firms have some ability to differentiate their product but there are no barriers to entry and there are a large number of firms, this will tend to drive profits toward zero in the long-run.

We model the "monopolistically competitive" firm as outlined below in Figure 12.1. Each firm has some ability to differentiate their product and thus faces downward sloping demand and marginal revenue curves. Firms will still optimize by choosing to produce the level of output where MC = MR. In the long-run profits will be zero, because if profits are greater than zero, more firms will enter the market. This will tend to drive the demand curve for each firm down until profits reach zero once again. Once this occurs, there will no longer be a tendency for new firms to enter the market and long-run equilibrium is established.

**Figure 12.1
Equilibrium for a Monopolistically
Competitive Firm**

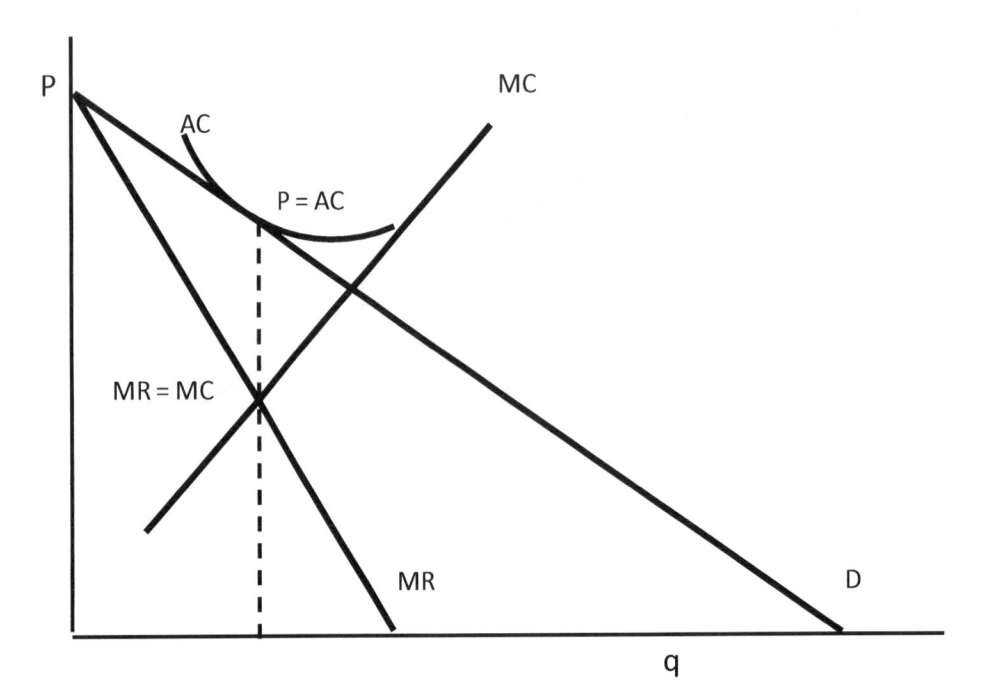

Practice Problems for Chapter 12

1. Draw the graphs for the long-run equilibriums for the monopolistically competitive firm and the perfectly competitive firm. Try not to refer to the text if possible. Discuss the similarities and differences between perfect and monopolistic competition.

2. What types of industries might be represented by monopolistic competition? Can you think of some real world examples?

Chapter 13

The Labor Market, Human Capital and Productivity

Determination of the Wage in the Competitive Equilibrium

Just as firms find the optimal level of output by setting MC = MR, they will tend to hire labor up until the point where the value of the output that is produced by a marginal worker is just equal to what the firm has to pay the worker, the wage (W). We define the ***value of the marginal product of labor*** as:

Eq. 13.1 $VMP_L = P \times MP_L$

Thus, the price times the marginal product of labor is the value of the marginal product of labor; it is the increment to output generated by an increment to labor, valued at market prices. Firms will hire worker up until the value of what they produce is equal to the wage. Thus, the VMP_L is really the demand curve for labor in Figure 13.1 below. The value of the marginal product of labor will equal the wage in equilibrium.

Figure 12.1
Demand for Labor Tied to Value of the Marginal Product of Labor

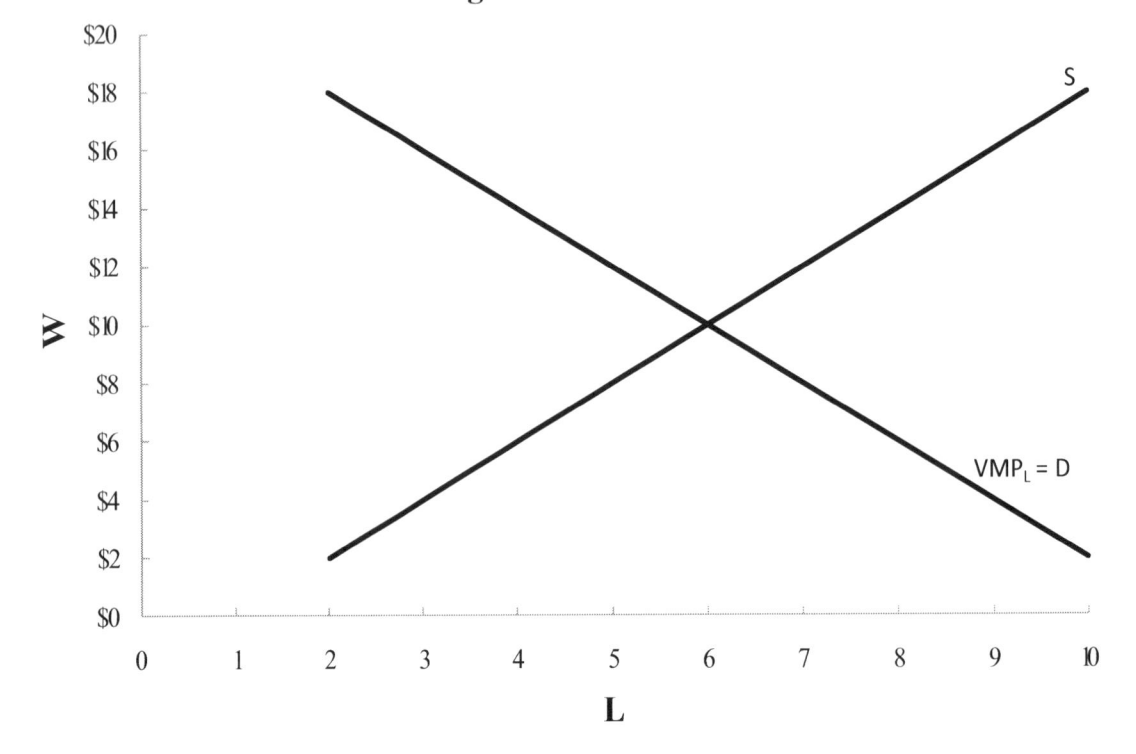

In a competitive industry in long-run equilibrium, the marginal cost is equal to the price. From above, the $VMP_L = W$ and since $MC = P$, using Eq. 13.1, $MC = W/MP_L$.

In Table 13.1 below, given a price of $2 per unit. The value of the marginal product of labor is $2 \times MP_L$. Given a wage of $10 per hour of labor, marginal cost is equal to $10/MP_L$.

Table 13.1

L	MP_L	VMP_L	MC
1	10	20	1
2	9	18	1.11
3	8	16	1.25
4	7	14	1.43
5	6	12	1.67
6	5	10	2

The firm would hire workers until the value of the marginal product of labor is set equal to the wage. In this case, it would hire 6 units of labor. The marginal cost is $2, which is also equal to the price of output, so $MC = MR = P$.

Raising Living Standards in a Market Economy

From these very simple relationships we discussed so far in this chapter, there are some important insights that can come out of it. If the wage is set equal to the value of the marginal product of labor in a market economy, if you want to raise the wage, you will have to raise the marginal product of labor. (Prices of output on most goods and services will be determined by supply and demand on a global level. Especially in a small country, the government would not have much ability to influence world prices.)

Gifts of charity can raise standards of living in the short-run, but to put a country on a path to development over time, there is no doubt that the average wage in a country will be the chief determinant of living standards within that country. In order to increase the wage, you have to increase the value of the marginal product of labor, and since in a small country prices are determined exogenously, this means you have in increase labor productivity and raise the marginal product of labor. There are really only two ways to do this: either increase human capital through education or increase physical capital to give workers more physical capital to work with, which would in turn raise labor productivity.

Thus, a small poor country will somehow have to attract more physical capital or increase its ability to educate its workforce if it wishes to raise living standards.

Raising Living Standards Over Time

We showed above that we need to increase labor productivity to increase living standards on a sustainable basis over time. There are two possible sources for the resources to be able to do this: 1) foreign sources and 2) domestic sources. If a country is able to generate savings, it will be able to accumulate capital which in turn will lead to greater labor productivity and wages over time. However, for a lot of poor countries it is very difficult to get its population to save. By definition, if people are living at a subsistence level, saving more might even make it difficult to survive! Thus, very poor countries probably must rely on foreign capital if they hope to raise living standards for their population. Either they need to attract investment dollars from abroad or receive aid that can be used to increase either physical capital or human capital through education.

Although the economics in this chapter is quite simple, the insights developed here are important. In a market economy where the wage is the chief determinant of living standards, somehow additional resources must be garnered to increase the marginal product of labor and improve wages and living conditions for the poor.

Practice Problem for Chapter 13

1. Suppose you are the benevolent dictator of a poor sub-Saharan African country. You want to permanently raise living standards in your country. Using the theory from this chapter, what do you need to do and how do you do it?

Chapter 14

Taxation Policy: Efficiency vs. Equity

In this chapter, we examine various aspects of tax policy. We will see that there are often conflicts between efficiency and equity. In other words, there are differences in tax systems that aim to maximize welfare/efficiency versus those aimed at correcting inequities such as an unequal income distribution.

Welfare Loss from a Specific Tax

We start by looking at the situation of a specific tax applied to the producers of a good. A specific tax of this sort has the effect of causing the supply curve to shift up and to the left. (See Figure 14.1 below.) Consumer surplus becomes area A, government revenue would be areas B + C, and producer surplus would be areas E + F. (The consumer sees the price P_c and the producer sees the price P_P after tax.) The deadweight loss from the tax would be equal to area D.

Figure 14.1
Deadweight Loss From a Specific Tax Paid By Producer

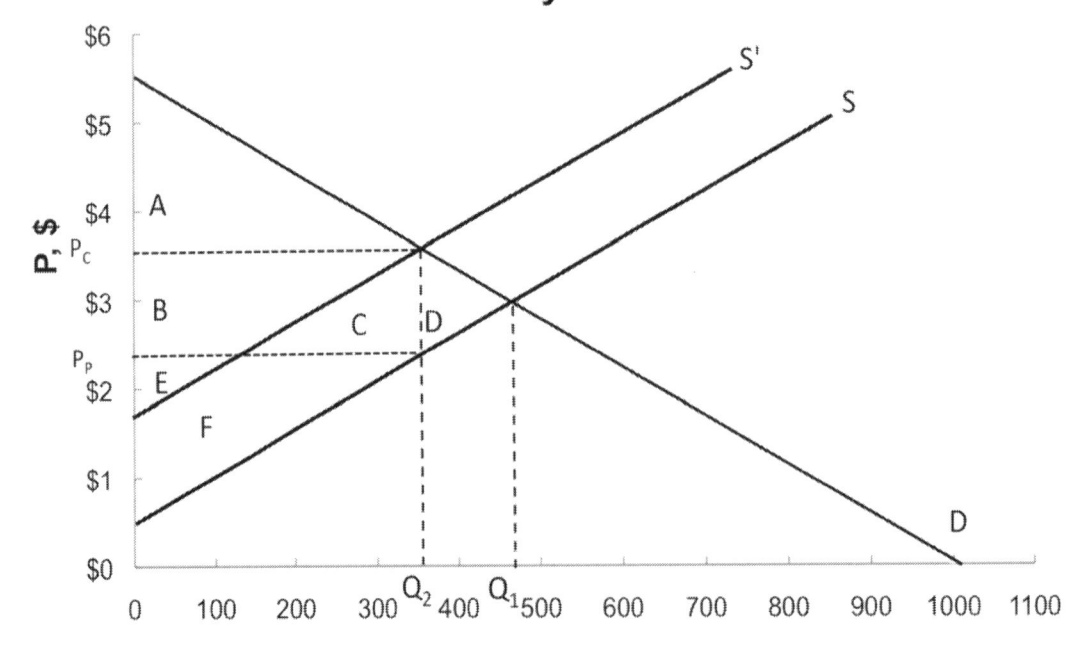

Looking at Figure 14.1 above, can you figure out the type of goods that would lead to the smallest deadweight loss from a specific tax? The answer is goods for which the elasticity of supply and demand is relatively inelastic. Right away we can see the tradeoff between efficiency and equity. For example, necessities tend to have more inelastic demand than luxury items. Poorer people would tend to spend a larger proportion of their income on necessities compared with wealthier people. Therefore, if the government was thinking of implementing a specific tax it would have to weigh the efficiency issues against issues of equity.

Government Revenue as a Share of GDP

Total government revenue as a share of GDP has been rising for the last 100 years or so. 100 years ago, government revenue as a share of GDP was something like 7 percent. Now it is close to 30 percent. This figure may continue to climb in upcoming years as the government strives to close the large government budget deficit it is currently running.

Table 14.1 shows the share of government revenue as a percentage of GDP in various countries.

Table 14.1

Total Government Revenue as a Share of GDP

Sweden	50%	United States	28%
France	45%	Japan	27%
United Kingdom	37%	Mexico	20%
Germany	36%	China	15%

Source: OECD. Data are for the most recent years available.

The federal government collects about 2/3 of the tax revenue in the US. Of all the tax revenue raised, the largest contributor to federal tax revenue is individual income taxes. The marginal tax rates for the income tax is outlined in Table 14.2 below.

Table 14.2

Selected Marginal Income Tax Rates in the US

Single Filing Status		Married Filing Jointly	
Income between 0 and $8350	10%	Income between 0 and $16700	10%
" " $8350 and 33950	15%	" " $16700 and 67900	15%
" " $33950 and 82250	25%	" " $67900 and 137050	25%
" over $372,950	35%	" over $372,950	35%

The US Federal Budget Deficit

When the federal government spends more than it receives in tax revenue, we say it is running a deficit. (The opposite would be called a surplus.) Right now, the government is on target for the largest federal budget deficit in history of about $1.4 trillion dollars in 2010 or nearly 10% of GDP. Moreover, with the aging of the baby boom generation—people born between about 1948 and 1965 or so—the government's challenge will be even greater in the years to come. Spending on social security and medicare (health spending for the aged) will inevitably rise as the baby boomers age. The government will either have to raise taxes or cut spending or the government's budget deficit could spiral out of control. The country Greece is now experiencing the pain and dislocations caused by an "out of whack" budget deficit problem; this could happen to the United States as well, if the president and Congress don't work together to reduce the government's budget deficit over time.

The problem with reducing spending for the federal government is that many of the most important categories of spending are considered almost untouchable---like social security, medicare, interest payments on the national defense, military spending, etc. The author expects that the government will have to raise tax rates on many if not most individuals as we move through the decade after 2010.

Other Possible Tax Systems

There are alternative systems of taxation to the "progressive" income tax system of the US. (By progressive, we mean that individuals who make more money pay higher tax rates. The opposite would be "regressive".)

Lump sum taxes—some individuals advocate getting rid of the progressive income tax structure with all of its special deductions and distortions caused by years of complex measures introduced into the tax code and replace it with a lump sum tax where everyone would pay the same amount. This would be more efficient and would reduce the hours spent preparing tax forms, but obviously it would fall most heavily on the poor and would be regressive in nature.

Flat tax—another scheme to simplify the tax structure is referred to as the flat tax. Everyone would pay the same marginal rate. Again, this would fall more heavily on poor people in the lower tax brackets.

Value-added taxes—luminaries such as the ex-Federal Reserve Chairman Paul Volcker have advocated implementing a system of value-added taxes as is common in parts of Europe. This could be like a national sales tax and again would likely be regressive in nature.

Negative income tax—this is a tax system designed to subsidize work effort. In this scheme, workers who earn less than a certain amount would be eligible to receive subsidies from the government to bring them up to a certain minimum standard of living. Although this tax scheme might require some initial outlays to implement, it could ultimately reduce spending in some areas like food stamps, welfare and even on incarcerating people. Usually a negative income tax system would be implemented with an elimination of the minimum wage. Thus, employment would probably go up as the real wage paid by firms goes down. (The federal government would, in effect, be subsidizing employment.) In the end, this could lead to a reduction in crime as unemployment comes down and more workers can find jobs. Also, spending on food stamps and welfare would likely decrease for the same reason.

Practice Problems for Chapter 14

1. What changes do you think should be implemented in the tax code? Could you suggest ways in which the tax could be made fairer or more efficient?

2. List the pros and cons for a negative income tax system as you see it. Would you be in favor of implementing a negative income tax?

Chapter 15

Government and the Market for Goods

Sometimes the market doesn't provide the optimal allocation of resources. For example, would the private sector be able to come up with private donors to donate lands for public parks. Who would pay for roads and national defense when needed?

One of the most important functions of government is to provide ***public goods***. We will define public goods in a very specific way soon, but for the time being one can think of public goods as the goods and services provided by government for public consumption, usually without a fee attached to it. Examples of public goods are elementary, middle school and high school education, national defense, roads/highways and public parks. In this chapter, we will study some of the issues surrounding the provision of public goods and other types of goods where the "free market" outcome may not be optimal and there may be a role for government in improving the allocation of resources.

Classifying Different Types of Goods

Economists have devised schemes to classify goods into different categories. They do this because they recognize that there may be different strategies to improve the allocation of resources for different types of goods and the free market by itself may not lead to the optimal allocation of resources.

The methodology that economists most commonly use to sort goods into their different categories is to ask two basic questions: 1) Are the goods ***rival in consumption***? and 2) Are the goods ***excludable***? By rival in consumption, we mean does my use or consumption of a good diminish your ability to use or consume that good. A public park would generally not be rival in consumption; my enjoyment of the park does not necessarily diminish your ability to enjoy the park. However, a candy bar would be rival in consumption. My eating of the candy bar effectively prohibits your ability to consume the candy bar. Excludable means that there is a means to limit use of a good or service. For example, a toll road excludes those who do not wish to pay or do not have the appropriate pass to use the road, whereas most roads do not feature excludability and are open to everyone with a car. A private lake is excludable, but oceans and other large bodies of water are generally not excludable.

Table 15.1 below shows examples of the various types of goods and also gives the names for each category.

Table 15.1

Types of Goods

Are the goods rival in consumption?

		YES	**NO**
		Private Goods	*Natural Monopolies*
Are the goods excludable?	**YES**	Candy bars	Police protection
		Fine wine	Wireless internet
		Sporting goods	Private clubs
		Common Resources	*Public Goods*
	NO	Fish in rivers and lakes	National parks
		Busy city streets	Uncrowded public schools
		Congested public schools	National defense

Private goods are excludable and rival in consumption. Probably most goods fall into this category. If I own a shirt or a candy bar, I will probably keep others from using it/them and I will probably not give the "shirt off my back" to other people. (I usually don't lend my clothing out, do you???)

Natural monopolies are excludable, (i.e., the Miami police work to protect people in Miami), but not rival. The police can protect a great number of people at the same time. Similarly, wireless internet can require a password to access a network, but multiple people can access a network at the same time.

Common resources are goods that are not excludable but are rival in consumption. This category creates some interesting challenges for public policy. If we allow our rivers and lakes to be fished without restriction, we may damage our ability to be able to enjoy future benefits from fishing in those rivers and lakes. How do we solve the problem of congestion at rush hour in our larger cities?

Public goods are goods that are not excludable, nor rival in consumption. Parks, national defense and public education are examples of public goods. The free market won't tend to provide these goods on its own.

The Free Rider Problem

The provision of public goods can sometimes serve to solve problems related to something called the "free rider problem". Suppose a public park tries to finance its operations through soliciting voluntary contributions from visitors. A sign posted at the park asks every visitor to contribute $3.00 per visit. Most likely, some people will pay each time they visit the park and others will choose not to pay, since there isn't any enforcement mechanism. The people who choose not to pay are known as *free riders*. To get around this problem, we generally tax the entire population and use some of these revenues to sustain public parks and do not charge admission to the parks.

Common Resources

Probably the most interesting category of good from a public policy perspective is the common resources category. There are frequently conflicts that arise due to this type of good. For example, in the southwestern United States water is a scarce resource. If farmers drain water from rivers and reservoirs to use for irrigation, there is less potable water to serve the major cities. Sometimes you have people in different states accessing the same sources of water. All of these issues create possible conflicts in resource utilization that need to be resolved or the sources of water can be drained down to suboptimal levels.

Practice Problems for Chapter 15

1. Categorize the following goods in the four basic categories (private goods, natural monopolies, public goods, common resources): fire protection, elite private colleges, public grazing pastures in Wyoming, congested toll roads, rural roads, personal hygiene items, federally subsidized research, economics tutoring services.

2. Choose a common resources problem that you think is critically important. Discuss mechanisms to improve the use of the common resource such that it would be better utilized for long-term enjoyment/use.

3. Discuss what types of public goods that you think are underprovided by the federal government and overprovided by the federal government. Suggest mechanisms that might help the federal government optimize the provision of public goods. How would you implement these mechanisms?

Chapter 16

Externalities and their Remedies

It's Saturday night and you head out to the local club to hear your favorite band, "Orange Smashers," which is an alternative, hard rock, indie band that plays music at 2000 decibels. You may really enjoy this band and appreciate that the last set starts at 2:00 am, but people living in the surrounding apartment buildings can still hear oranges being smashed at 4:00 in the morning and don't appreciate the sound effects.

In economics terms, Orange Smashers produce ***externalities***, which are the side effects or unintended impacts of various forms of activity on bystanders. Orange Smashers aren't the only ones who produce externalities; nuclear power facilities that warm the waters of the surrounding oceans or lakes on which they are situated, chemical plants that produce hazardous chemicals and emit toxic fumes, garbage pickup trucks that wake people in residential neighborhoods are all examples of externalities. Anything that is an unintended side effect of an economic activity is an externality.

Externalities can sometimes be positive. When I was in college, I worked summers at the Ravinia Music Festival in Highland Park, Illinois, a suburb of Chicago. The Chicago Symphony Orchestra played regularly at Ravinia. Classical music aficionados might choose to buy a house near Ravinia in order to be able to hear the sounds of the CSO for free. Some people might enjoy the smell of cookies and pastries if they live near a bakery. (However, others might complain about the negative externalities of rodents if the bakery doesn't clean up after itself.)

It is probably true that people who stay in school and get an advanced education are less likely to commit crimes than individuals who do not continue with their education. If this is true, it may make sense to subsidize public education, and in fact, we do!

Economists attempt to measure the costs and benefits of externalities as can be seen in Figure 16.1 below. Externalities, where measurable, should be added to the normal market-based supply and demand curves. Where there are negative externalities, these costs should be added to the private cost (which is represented by the supply curve). Positive

Figure 16.1 - A

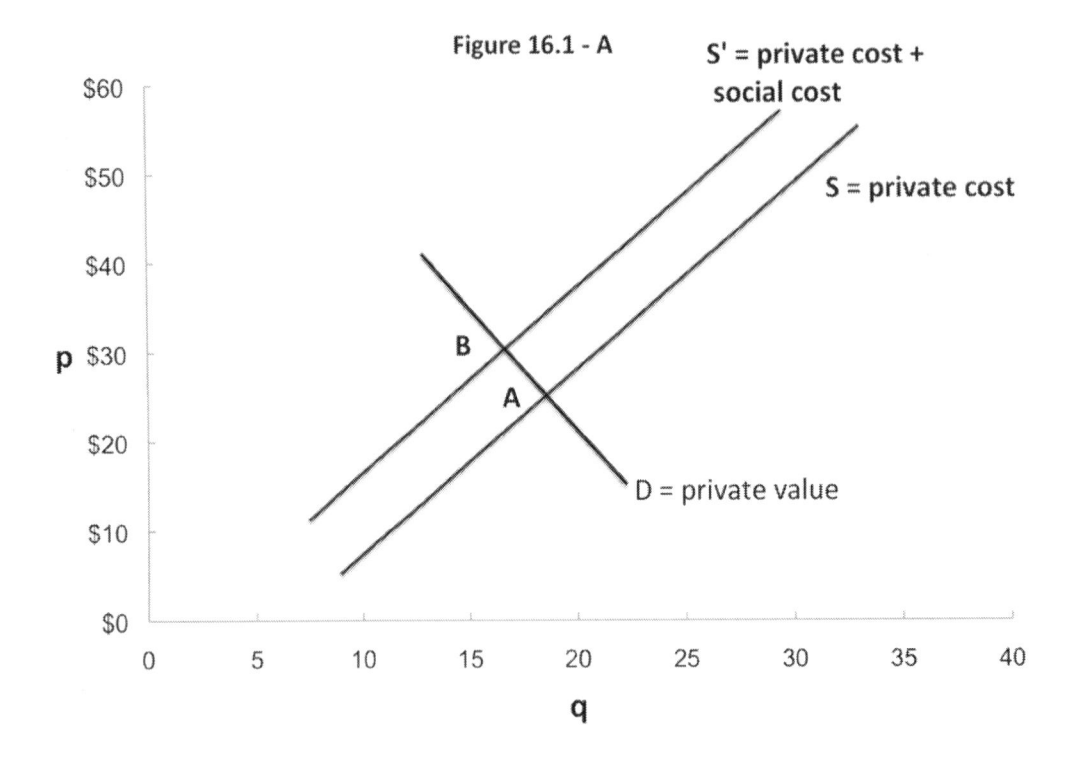

- S' = private cost + social cost
- S = private cost
- D = private value

Figure 16.1 - B

- S = private cost
- D' = private value + social value
- D = private value

16.2

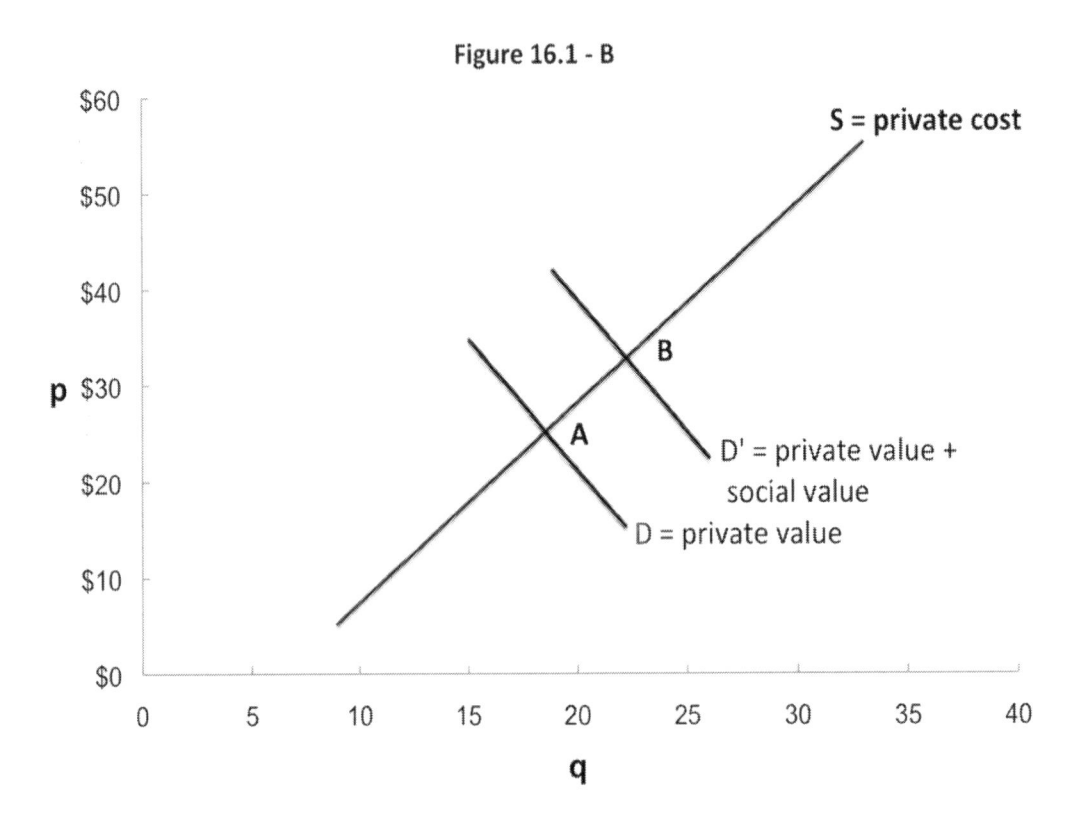

externalities should be added to the private value to come up with the social value. Thus, negative externalities should shift the supply curve up and to the left and positive externalities, if properly accounted for, would tend to shift demand up and to the right.

Pigouvian Taxes and Subsidies

Economist Arthur Pigou (1877 to 1959) is generally credited with the idea that the government should implement a series of corrective taxes and subsidies to try to move the economy closer to the social optimum. "Pigouvian" taxes and subsidies are taxes and subsidies that are supposed to encourage economic actors to "internalize the externality" or bear the cost or benefit of the tax or subsidy such that they have the incentive to move closer to the social optimum.

The trouble with implementing a system of Pigouvian taxes and subsidies is the problem of accurately measuring the social costs and benefits from various externalities and then coming up with the appropriate system to encourage more appropriate economic behavior.

For example, let's suppose releasing steam as a byproduct of an industrial process reduces visibility in an urban area. How do we measure what the value of that reduction in visibility comes to? One could devise surveys and ask people what it is worth to them, but how easy is it to assign a dollar value to clear visibility? I am not sure that my own answer to that question would be the same every time someone asked me to assign a value to visibility.

But recognizing that placing a value on externalities is difficult does not mean that it is not worth the effort. The recent oil spill in the Gulf of Mexico is generating massive externalities in industries such as tourism and fishing, as well as reducing the quality of life for many individuals who live along the shore who enjoy using the beach and waterfront. Almost everyone would agree that the companies participating in the drilling of the well that is spewing the oil should bear much, if not all, of the cost of the cleanup, and maybe even be penalized financially as well.

The Coase Theorem

Ronald Coase is an economist associated with the University of Chicago that developed a theorem that says that if private parties can bargain over resource allocation at no cost, then the private market will be able to effectively solve the problems associated with externalities and efficiently allocate resources.

Going back to the Orange Smashers example from the beginning of the chapter, the Coase theorem would say that the neighbors of the club that hired the Orange Smashers could organize themselves and maybe threaten to stage demonstrations in front of the club to discourage people from attending their concerts. Or they could raise funds to pay the club owner to entice him/her to end the evenings' festivities a bit earlier. In any event, according to Coase, they should be able to bargain back and forth and reach a more equitable outcome, without the need for government interference. What do you think? Would that work generally?

Practice Problems for Chapter 16

1. What externalities do you perceive arise from the fact that emergency rooms at hospitals will generally not turn away poor people in need of care even if they do not have health insurance? Could you use the idea of Pigouvian taxes and subsidies to improve the allocation of health care services from a social perspective?

2. Try to draw a graph to illustrate the following externalities from a social cost or benefit perspective. (Hint: look at the example of Figure 16.1.)

   a) A chemical plant is emitting harmful toxins into the air.
   b) Popular stores can bring economic activity into an area and lead to job creation.
   c) Leading universities in math and science create growth poles for technology firms in the areas around the universities.
   d) Eating a healthy diet reduces obesity and demands on the national health care system.

3. John's rock band rehearses in a garage in a residential neighborhood until late into the night. Do you think the Coase theorem will apply here and that the relevant parties will be able to reach the socially optimal outcome through bargaining? Should there be government involvement in the outcome? Could you use Pigouvian taxes and subsidies to reach a better outcome?

4. True or false:

   a) Pigouvian taxes on polluters have to be weighed against the welfare loss from the tax.
   b) Positive externalities are generally associated with rising tax revenues for government authorities.
   c) It is obvious that creating a new airport for a city will only generate negative externalities.

Chapter 17

International Trade

In this final chapter, we analyze the societal benefits of trade and explore the impact of barriers to trade.

First, let's discuss the welfare impact of moving from a situation of ***autarky***, a situation where there is no trade, to free trade in the case of the automobile industry. Then we will analyze the further impact of a tariff and other trade barriers.

In Figure 17.1 below, the autarky equilibrium is at the point of intersection of the domestic demand and supply curves. Consumer surplus

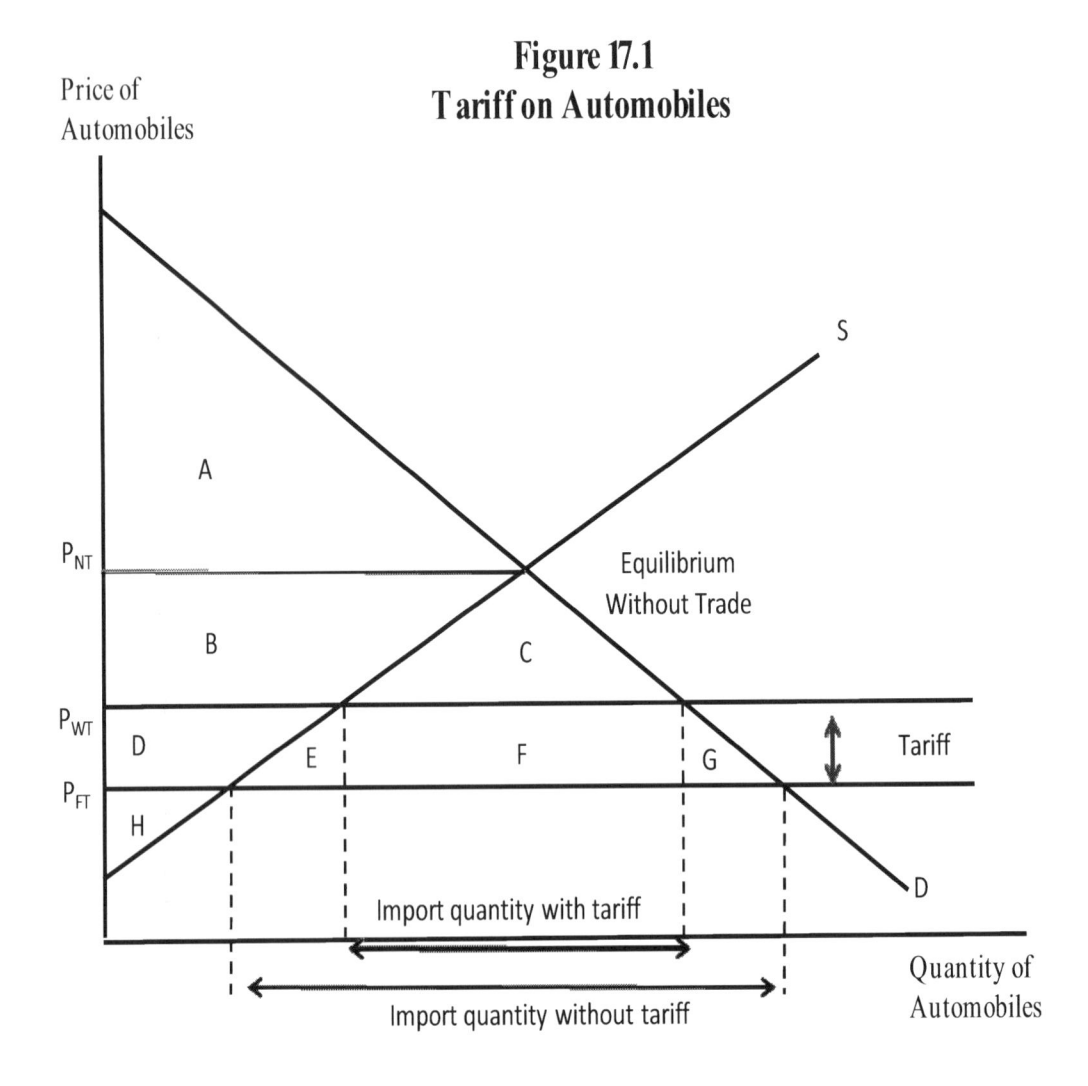

**Figure 17.1
Tariff on Automobiles**

17.1

is represented by area A and producer surplus by areas B + D + H. In this case, the free trade price for cars is below the domestic autarky price ($P_{FT} < P_{NT}$). With a move to free trade, consumer surplus increases to areas A + B + C + D + E + F + G, whereas producer surplus shrinks to H. Welfare increases by C + E + F + G.

This shows the great benefit that can be achieved by moving from a situation of autarky to a situation of free trade.

	(1) Without Trade	(2) Free Trade	(2) – (1) Change
Consumer Surplus	A	A+B+C+D +E+F+G	B+C+D+E +F+G
Producer Surplus	B+D+H	H	- B - D
Welfare	A+B+D+H	A+B+C+D+E+F +G+H	C+E+F+G

Now, let's analyze moving from free trade to a regime of trade but with a tariff imposed. In this case, welfare declines. We see from the analysis below that welfare declines by areas E + G.

	(1)	(2)	(2) – (1)
	Without Tariff	With Tariff	Change
Consumer Surplus	A+B+C+D +E+F+G	A+B+C	- D - E - F - G
Producer Surplus	H	D + H	D
Government Revenue	0	F	F
Welfare	A+B+C+D +E+F+G+H	A+B+C+D +H+F	- E - G

Suppose instead of a tariff, the government imposed an equivalent ***quota*** on imports of automobiles. This means the government would license an importer to import the same quantity of autos as would be imported under the tariff regime. In this case the analysis would be identical except the area representing government revenue would go to the holder of the import license and not the government. From the average citizens perspective, this would probably be a worse outcome than the tariff because the revenue goes to a private individual and not the government, but everything else is identical.

Let's consider one more case. Suppose the foreign exporters of cars to the United States are asked to restrict their exports to the amount of imports under the tariff regime above. (This is called a ***voluntary export restraint***.) Again, the analysis would be the same as the quota and the tariff, but the area F would go to the foreign auto exporter and not to the government. Again, welfare in the US would be lower than in the tariff situation.

Practice Problem for Chapter 17

1. Analyze the welfare impact of moving from autarky to free trade when the international free trade price is above the autarky price (P_{NT} in Figure 17.1 above.)

Afterword

The author hopes you have enjoyed this exploration of introductory microeconomic theory. We have developed insights into a number of important economic problems and issues. Further study in economics will focus on macroeconomic theory and more advanced micro and macro theory. Macroeconomics deals with the larger economic units of society and the economy as a whole. It employs different models and analytical techniques than those used here and, for many students, it may appear to be more relevant as it analyzes a lot of the important issues that appear in the newspapers on a daily basis like economic growth, unemployment, and inflation. Good luck in your future studies!

Made in the USA
Charleston, SC
19 January 2012